COLL

HENRY REED was born in B~~i~~. ~~g ——— ... .~~914 and educated at King
Edward VI Grammar School and Birmingham University. After a
period of teaching and freelance writing, he was conscripted into the
Royal Army Ordnance Corps in 1941. In 1942 he was transferred to the
Government Code and Cypher School at Bletchley Park. In the
evenings he wrote much of his first radio play, *Moby Dick* (1947), and
many of the poems later published in his first and only collection, *A Map
of Verona* (1946). In the mid-1950s Reed began to concentrate on writing
radio plays. His broadcast work includes two plays about Giacomo
Leopardi, a poet with whom he strongly identified: *The Unblest* (1949)
and *The Monument* (1950). In 1951 his play *The Streets of Pompeii* was
awarded the Italia Prize. Best known today, though, are his six plays fea-
turing his comic creation Hilda Tablet. Reed also worked as a fiction and
poetry reviewer for the *Listener* and the *New Statesman* and published
translations. His verions of Leopardi's poems were broadcast by the
BBC in 1975. He died in December 1986 and his *Collected Poems* were
published posthumously in 1991.

JON STALLWORTHY was educated at Rugby School, in the Royal West
African Frontier Force, and at Magdalen College, Oxford, where he
won the Newdigate Prize for Poetry. His books include eight collections
of poems, two critical studies of Yeats's poetry, *The Penguin Book of Love
Poetry*, *The Oxford Book of War Poetry*, editions of Wilfred Owen's *Complete
Poems and Fragments*, and *War Poems*, and two biographies: *Wilfred Owen*
(which won the Duff Cooper Memorial Prize, the W.H. Smith Literary
Award and the E.M. Forster Award), and *Louis MacNeice* (which won the
Southern Arts Literary Prize). In 1998 he published *Rounding the Horn:
Collected Poems* and his autobiography, *Singing School*. He has been a pro-
fessor of English Literature at Cornell and Oxford universities, and is
now a Senior Research Fellow of Wolfson College, Oxford, and a
Fellow of the British Academy.

SIR FRANK KERMODE taught English at Manchester, London and Cam-
bridge universities, as well as at Harvard, Yale and Columbia. He has
published widely on literature.

Photograph of Henry Reed c. 1949, from the University of
Birmingham Special Collections Department.
Reproduced by permission of the Royal Literary Fund.

HENRY REED

COLLECTED POEMS

Edited with an introduction by
JON STALLWORTHY

With a foreword by
FRANK KERMODE

CARCANET

First published in Great Britain by Oxford University Press (Oxford Poets) in 1991

This paperback edition first published in Great Britain in 2007 by
Carcanet Press Limited
Alliance House
Cross Street
Manchester M2 7AQ

A CIP catalogue record for this book is available from the British Library
ISBN 978 1 85754 943 0

The publisher acknowledges financial assistance from Arts Council England

Printed and bound in England by SRP Ltd, Exeter

... *T'acqueta omai. Dispera*
L'ultima volta. Al gener nostro il fato
Non donò che il morire. Omai disprezza
Te, la natura, il brutto
Poter che, ascoso, a comun danno impera,
E l'infinita vanità del tutto.

Giacomo Leopardi, from *A se stesso*

ACKNOWLEDGEMENTS

DOUGLAS CLEVERDON ended his obituary of Henry Reed, published in the *Independent* of 11 December 1986: 'To sort out the chaos [of his manuscripts] will be a major task.' So it proved, but the task fell into the hands of Catharine Carver who, characteristically, converted a Herculean labour into a labour of love. From 'the Box' of Reed's literary remains, she sorted the publishable drafts and fragments from the all too many unpublishable, exhumed uncollected poems and translations from the yellowing strata of magazine cuttings, dated them all and collated published texts with the author's corrected copies, and drafted the notes for this edition. For this she deserves the thanks not only of the editor but of every reader of this book. Thanks are due as well to Ann Colcord, who provided valuable advice and assistance over Reed's translations from the Italian; to Dr Roger Savage for sharing his unrivalled knowledge of Reed's published texts; to Sarah Berg, who prepared the initial hand-list of the contents of 'the Box'; and to Susan Westwood for liaison with the BBC's archives.

For assistance with the biographical section of the Introduction, I am grateful to the poet's niece, Mrs Jane Henrietta Reed, and to his literary executor, Mr John Tydeman; also to Professor Walter Allen and Mr Michael Ramsbotham.

JON STALLWORTHY
Wolfson College, Oxford
October 1990

CONTENTS

CONTENTS

PART V   Translations, Imitations (1949–1975)

PART VI   Early poems, drafts and fragments (1935–1986)

FOREWORD

HENRY REED was a sad man but a funny man, and his poems are funny or sad – often, as in the celebrated 'Lessons of the War', both at once. I first met him in 1965, in the office of Robert Heilman, then the benevolent but firm head of the English Department at the University of Washington in Seattle. Calling to present my credentials, I walked into a row: Heilman benevolently firm, Reed furious, licensed to be furious. He was in Seattle as a replacement for Theodore Roethke, the regular poet in residence, who had suddenly died. Whether Roethke had contributed to the routine work of the department I don't know, but if he hadn't Heilman did not regard this immunity as a precedent and was requiring Reed to give some lectures on the Brontës. Reed argued that he had been hired exclusively as a poet and declined to speak of these tiresome women. I came in when was telling Heilman this, and also scolding him for referring to the novelists by the fancy name their father had affected in order to suggest a connection with Lord Nelson. 'How can you ask me to lecture on the O'Prunty's?' he shouted. But he did as he was asked. He and Heilman were, or became, great friends.

The secretary of the department had an affluent businessman husband, and they had taken Henry under their protection, driving him around in one or other of their Thunderbirds, labelled 'His' and 'Hers'. Once we all went to lunch in the revolving restaurant on top of the Space Needle, and when our hosts left to get on with their work they left us slowly spinning there, with plenty of champagne to get us through the December afternoon. Henry, having been funny, now grew sad, holding up a bottle and contemplating the label, Mumms Extra Dry: 'Poor baby!' he sighed. The conversation sinking into melancholia, I quoted the advice of Thoreau, 'Do not be betrayed into a vulgar sadness,' but he rejected it, pointing out that Thoreau's crown of Thoreaus was remembering happier things. (He liked puns: Stallworthy points out that the epigraph to 'Lessons of the War' – *vixi duellis nuper idoneus / et militavi non sine gloria* – substitutes *duellis*, 'wars', for Horace's *puellis*, 'girls'. This is a better pun than the Seattle ones, especially as it subtly emphasises the heterosexuality of the implied author of 'Lessons of the War'.) Later in that lost day we found ourselves in a deplorable bar, where we were set upon by the resident *puellae*. 'Surely they can tell

I'm homosexual,' he said as if puzzled, though quite how they could be expected to do so was obscure to me, and anyway there were ample other reasons for abstinence. The girls must have wondered what we doing there, but so did we.

Back in London I would sometimes get back home after a hard day at the office and find him already there. He would invariably ask for Mozart and we would listen to one of the piano concertos. And he would invariably be moved as if coming upon a wonder for the first time: 'Exquisite,' he would murmur. 'Who's the pianist?' 'Still Ingrid Haebler, I'm afraid.' Around eleven he would ask to be poured into a taxi, and so the evening would end with a long chilly wait at the rank in Rosslyn Hill.

I don't remember much of his conversation on these occasions, except that he sometimes lamented his association with what had been the Third Programme. Much of his writing had been for radio: it included the successful series of comic programmes, seven in all, about the composeress Hilda Tablet and her associates; an adaptation of *Moby-Dick*; and many translations, including some plays of Betti that were very well thought of at the time. The editor has exhumed good verse from *Moby Dick* and from some of the others, verse remarkable for its fertility and density, but in the Sixties it was hard to imagine a bright future for radio drama. Some of his translations reached the stage, but Reed was not cut out for television.

He was gentle, melancholy and funny, and without conscious effort gave one a strong sense of his unaffected dedication to poetry, not least to Italian poetry; and also tacitly but powerfully, a sense that his life, though marked by a good deal of idiosyncratic achievement, was radically disappointing. Stallworthy remarks that he has lost his way, or his way back, to the great good place that makes fairly frequent appearances in his verse; it is there, figured as Verona, in the first poem of his early collection. It is re-imagined in a remarkable poem called 'The Changeling' which appeared in the *Listener* early in 1950. After many vicissitudes a man at last reaches the destination he has always thought proper to him:

> And comes, at last, to stand
> On his scented evening lawn
> Under his flowering limes
> Where dim in the dusk and high,
> His mansion is proudly set,

And the single light burns
In the room where his sweet young wife
Waits in his ancient bed.
The stable clock chimes.
And he to his house draws near,
And on the threshold turns,
With a silent glance to convey
Up to his summer sky,
Where his first pale stars appear:
All this is false. And I
Am an interloper here.

In another fine poem, hitherto unpublished, 'The Château' ('Yet will I
fear no evil: not even here'), the theme recurs as it were in the major, and
the excluded figure is imagined as finally entering his own domain and
discovering that the time of exclusion, properly understood, was part of
his total felicity. He approaches his 'own and veritable door':

I shall open it, enter, and learn
That in all this hungry time I have never wanted,
But have, elsewhere, on honey and milk been fed,
Have in green pastures somewhere lain, and in the mornings,
Somewhere beside still waters have
Mysteriously, ecstatically, been led.

A Map of Verona was published in 1946, when Reed was in his early thir-
ties, and it stood alone, though Douglas Cleverdon produced a fine
limited edition of 'Lessons of the War', designed and printed by Will and
Sebastian Carter, in 1970. Another collection, to be called *The Auction
Sale, and Other Poems*, was promised in 1977 but never appeared. Reed left
certain pencilled instructions on his manuscripts which suggest that he
was expecting or hoping for a *Collected Poems*, and this we now have,
thanks to Catherine Carver, who sorted out the heaps of drafts, clip-
pings and corrections left by the poet, and Jon Stallworthy, who has
made this a model edition of a modern poet, with adequate textual and
bibliographical annotation, and a useful biographical introduction.

He can justly claim that the result dispels the 'gross misperception' of
Reed, author of 'The Naming of Parts', as a one-poem poet. He is
always refined, calculated, expert, and nearly always alive with his sad-
nesses. Stallworthy does him a slight injustice by prefixing as an

epigraph some very gloomy verses by Leopardi (*l'infinita vanità del tutto*), quite rightly pointing out that Reed had a special attachment to Leopardi – he wrote two plays about him and translated several of his poems: but I find these poems the least impressive in the volume. Leopardi feeds too directly into Reed's deep reservoir of gloom, and the translations, unlike the original poems, somehow sound rather inert. One of them, 'The Broom', reminds one a little of the Arnold of 'Empedocles on Etna', rejected by its author as altogether too glum.

There was always this danger. On lighter occasions he sometimes sounds more like a less dandyish Clough. But the strongest influence, hardly surprising in a younger poet of his time, was Eliot. Stallworthy reminds us that the celebrated parody of Eliot, 'Chard Whitlow', was written before 'Little Gidding', but the cadences of Eliot, the rhythms of the earlier Quartets, mimicked there with such absurd accuracy, were always in Reed's head.

> Waking to find the room not as I thought it was,
> But the window further away, and the door in another direction

is as close to Eliot, though unparodically, as 'Chard Whitlow'. So, in another mode, is this, from one of Reed's dramatic monologues, 'Philoctetes':

> The noiseless chant has begun in the heart of the wound,
> The heavy procession of pain along the nerve.

It may be worth adding that the influence seems least assimilated when Reed must have been working fast, for the radio: in the verses from *Pytheas* (1947), here printed for the first time, the master too audibly presides over all. And somewhere behind Reed's dream allegories lurk 'Gerontion' and *The Waste Land*. But he was also intimate with Hardy, and worked for a long time on a biography before giving it up; his narrative poem 'The Auction Sale', though very individual, and ending with the characteristic exclusion from delight, is in Hardy's manner. Finally there are, no doubt inevitably, echoes of Auden, too.

Yet he holds his own note. 'Outside and In', a fine early poem, strikes it: intense apprehension at the prospect of a fate one would endure rather than protract. A fine late poem, 'Three Words' (too highly wrought for quotation except in its entirety), has the lexical agility of 'The Naming of Parts'; it is as witty, but in a sense excluding laughter.

'The Town Itself' and 'The Blissful Land' revisit in terminal sadness the lost Verona – 'I had not known that the weather, in what seemed, / At first, unchangeably sought out by the sun, / Could be so variable... I have come to a place where I have nothing to give' – and its counterpart, that lost blissful land which, once entered, would make all torments and losses the themes of a present delight ('It wasn't you that he wanted! How dared you to come here alone?'). Finally there is the resigned, elegantly executed signing-off little allegory called 'L'Envoi'. Reed certainly earned his 'Collected'. Stallworthy is right to claim distinction for these poems, and it can be seen the more clearly by his having brought them together.

FRANK KERMODE

This is an edited version of an article which first appeared in *The London Review of Books*, Vol. 13 No. 23, December 1991
www.lrb.co.uk

INTRODUCTION

I

THE author of 'Naming of Parts', probably the most anthologized English poem of the Second World War, has too often been held to be that and that only. Like Julian Grenfell, author of 'Into Battle', he is seen as the saddest freak of the literary fairground: the one-poem poet. This book gives the lie to that gross misperception.

Henry Reed was born, in Birmingham, on 22 February 1914 and named after his father, a master brick-layer and foreman in charge of forcing at Nocks' Brickworks. Henry senior was nothing if not forceful, a serious drinker and womanizer, who as well as his legitimate children fathered an illegitimate son who died during the Second World War. In this, he may have been following ancestral precedent: family legend had it that the Reeds were descended from a bastard son of an eighteenth- or nineteenth-century Earl of Dudley. Henry senior's other enthusiasms included reading, but the literary abilities of his son Henry junior seem, paradoxically, to have been inherited from a mother who was illiterate. Born Mary Ann Ball, the eldest child of a large family that had migrated from Tipton to Birmingham, she could not be spared from her labours at home during what should have been her schooldays, and when, in her late middle age, her granddaughter tried, unsuccessfully, to teach her to read, she wept with frustration and shame. Mary Ann Reed had a remarkable memory, however, and a well-stocked repertoire of fairy-stories—told with great verve—and songs to enchant her children and grandchild.

A daughter, Gladys, born in 1908, was encouraged to make the most of the schooling her mother had not had. She was a good student and in due course became a good teacher, discovering her vocation in teaching her younger brother. Gladys played a crucial role in the education of Henry (or Hal, as he was known in the family, a name perhaps borrowed from Shakespeare's hero) and was to become and remain the most important woman in his life. He was not an easy child. On one occasion dismembering his teddy bear, he buried its head, limbs, and torso around the garden and went howling to his mother. She was obliged to exhume the scattered parts, wash, and reassemble them for the little tyrant. At the state primary school in Erdington, he clashed with a hated teacher who pronounced him educationally subnormal. A psychiatrist was called in and, having examined the child, claimed to have detected promise of mathematical genius.

Moving on to King Edward VI Grammar School in Aston, Reed specialized in Classics. Since Greek was not taught, he taught himself, and went on to win the Temperley Latin prize and a scholarship to Birmingham University. There he was taught and befriended—as were his Birmingham contemporaries Walter Allen and Reggie Smith—by a young Lecturer in the Classics Department, Louis MacNeice. Reed had a remarkable speaking voice and a gift for mimicry (and for assuming the accents of a class not his own), and as an undergraduate, he acted in and produced plays, which may have led to his career in radio; in any case, for the rest of his life he delighted in the company of actors—partly perhaps because he was acting a part himself: that of the debonair, even aristocratic, literary man about town.

He gained a first-class degree at Birmingham in 1934 and wrote a notable thesis on Thomas Hardy, leaving the University two years later as its youngest MA. Like most of his Birmingham contemporaries, he had so far lived at home, but was not a happy member of the household. Hal was ashamed of his parents, or so they felt, and only his sister Gladys had much sympathy for the elegant butterfly struggling to break free from the Brummagem chrysalis. There was another factor, though how much Reed's parents knew of this is uncertain: he had had his first sexual, homosexual, experience when he was nineteen, and later had a tormented affair with a boy who developed paranoia. It was clearly time for him to leave home.

Like many other writers of the Thirties, he tried teaching—at his old school—and, again like most of them, hated it and left to make his way as a freelance writer and critic. He began the research for a full-scale life of Thomas Hardy, and his father financed a first trip to Italy. There he was taken to the ample bosom of a Neapolitan family he found more congenial than his own and would later celebrate in a radio play, *Return to Naples* (1950). Before he could himself return, Mussolini had to be overthrown, and in the summer of 1941 a Hal much less heroic than Shakespeare's was conscripted into the Royal Army Ordnance Corps. On 10 July, he wrote to his sister (now Mrs Winfield and the mother of a daughter, Jane):

We have begun our departmental training—which means that army train-ing has to be concentrated into 5/8 of the day, and is therefore increasing in savagery. This blitztraining is, to my mind, absurd. The R.A.O.C. lost 10% of its personnel in Belgium, through being noncombatant. They aim, there-fore, at making us combatant, in 9 weeks; at the end of that time we are expected to be able to shoot accurately, to manage a bren gun, an anti-tank gun & various other kinds, to use a bayonet, to throw hand-grenades & whatnot and to fire at aircraft. I do not think the management of a tank is included in the course, but pretty well everything else is.

Our departmental training, some of which is an official secret, known only to the British & German armies, has consisted mainly of learning the strategic disposition of the R.A.O.C. in the field: this is based, not, as I feared, on the Boer War, but on the Franco-Prussian War of 1871. It is taught by lecturers who rarely manage to conceal their dubiety at what they are teaching. But it is restful after the other things, & we are allowed to attend in P.T. 'kit'. This is nicely balanced by the fact that we attend P.T. wearing *all* our 'kit', except blankets. (I will never call a child of mine Christopher.)

The same letter gives, incidentally, a clear view of the left-wing political position that Reed, for all his aristocratic fantasies, was never to abandon: 'I hope', he wrote, 'a good deal from Russia, of course, but rather joylessly: the scale of it all is beyond my grasp, & it is terrible to see a country which, with all its faults, has been alone in working to give the fruits of labour to the people who have earned them, thus attacked . . .'

Reed served—'or rather *studied*', as he preferred to put it—in the Ordnance Corps until 1942 when, following a serious bout of pneumonia and a prolonged convalescence, he was transferred to the Government Code and Cypher School at Bletchley. At first he was employed as a cryptographer in the Italian Section, but was subsequently moved to the Japanese Section where he learned the language and worked as a translator. In the evenings he wrote much of his first radio play, *Moby Dick*, and many of the poems later to be published in *A Map of Verona*. It was not a life he would have chosen, but it had its compensations: security, time for his own work, and the start of an important—perhaps his most important—friendship.

Michael Ramsbotham was also a writer, five years younger than Henry Reed, and from a more privileged background. After

Charterhouse, from which he was expelled, he went up to King's College, Cambridge. At the end of his second year, in June 1940, he was called up and given a commission in the RNVR. His active service ended in September 1941, when he was posted to the Italian Section of Naval Intelligence at Bletchley. In 1943, he and Reed would sometimes escape the monotony of the canteen for a civilian lunch in Leighton Buzzard. The following year, they went on leave together twice to Charleston, a little fishing harbour near St Austell in Cornwall. Reed by this time had lost all trace of his Birmingham accent and acquired a somewhat Sitwellian manner. A quick wit and a staggering memory—especially for Shakespeare—made him an engaging companion.

On VJ Day 1945, he was demobbed. A few weeks earlier, Ramsbotham had suffered a nervous breakdown and went absent without leave, taking himself off to North Cornwall where, after a month or two, Reed joined him. Later both men were recalled to the Service. Reed, adopting Nelson's tactics, declined to see the signal, and the Navy let the matter drop. Ramsbotham was posted to the Staff of the Commander-in-Chief, Portsmouth, and during the following autumn and winter commuted, whenever he was off duty, from Portsmouth to Dorchester where Reed was living at the Antelope Hotel, continuing his research for the Hardy biography.

In April 1946, Ramsbotham was demobbed and they celebrated with a holiday in Ireland, the highlight of which was a happy fortnight as guests of Elizabeth Bowen at Bowen's Court. Returning to England in July, they briefly rented a house in Charleston, but soon moved to another rented house, Lovells Farm, in Marnhull, Dorset—Hardy's Marlot—where Ramsbotham worked on a novel while Reed reviewed fiction and poetry for the *Listener* and the *New Statesman* and worked on Hardy. His first and only collection of poems, *A Map of Verona*, dedicated to Ramsbotham, was published in London that year (1946) by Jonathan Cape, and in New York the following year by Reynal & Hitchcock. In January 1947 the two-hour radio adaptation of Melville's novel *Moby Dick* was produced by the BBC, and published the same year, again by Cape.

By February 1948, however, the atmosphere at Lovells Farm had become too emotionally claustrophobic for Ramsbotham and he walked out—leaving a note—but by April had returned, and the two set off for a long holiday in Cyprus. The following February,

Reed rented Gable Court, a large sixteenth-century house with Victorian additions in the Dorset village of Yetminster, where he continued his research for the life of Hardy and wrote two fine verse plays about another poet whose work he was translating and with whom he identified strongly, Giacomo Leopardi: *The Unblest* (1949) and *The Monument* (1950). The year at Gable Court, for Reed the best of times, was followed by the worst of times. In February 1950 the couple split up, Reed leaving his Eden (as it would, increasingly, seem to him) for London, where he was to live for the rest of his life, apart from terms as a Visiting Professor of Poetry at the University of Washington, Seattle, in 1964, 1965–6, and 1967, and occasional trips to Europe.

Perhaps in search of an earlier happiness, Reed had returned to Italy in July 1951, heading for Verona, 'the small strange city' lovingly imagined in the title-poem of his first book:

> one day I shall go.
> The train will bring me perhaps in utter darkness
> And drop me where you are blooming, unaware
> That a stranger has entered your gates, and a new devotion
> Is about to attend and haunt you everywhere.

A letter to his parents suggests that his prophecy had been fulfilled: 'It is a most lovely city,' he wrote, 'small enough for me to walk right across it in less than an hour; I had a letter of introduction to a friend of a friend & was in consequence well looked after & made much fuss of. My arrival was even announced on the radio, I learned with much delight later on.' It was a successful holiday and resulted in one of the best of Reed's radio plays on Italian themes, *The Streets of Pompeii*, awarded an Italia Prize in 1951. Much of his work for the BBC Features Department was commissioned and produced by Douglas Cleverdon, who wrote of him in his obituary (the *Independent*, 11 December 1986):

In these Italian pieces Henry Reed revealed his instinctive mastery of the art of radio. All his creative powers were brought into play. For he was not only a poet of great sensibility; he had also a lively sense of comedy and of the absurd, and a remarkable gift for dramatic invention. He could be extremely witty, both in his social life and in his radio writing; and the wit could overflow into satire and occasionally malice. Yet, though homosexual by nature, he had an extraordinary sympathy with women's most profound emotions, and could portray them with tenderness and under-standing . . .

His scripts were rarely completed more than a day or two before rehearsals began, but he particularly relished the affectionate esteem in which he was held by the group of players who usually formed the nucleus of his cast. As he usually attended all rehearsals, this affection was enhanced during the later stages of his radio career, when the poetic content of his work was gradually overtaken by the hilariously satirical.

In the mid-Fifties, Reed made a major liberating decision: he abandoned the biography of Hardy, which for years had burdened him with guilt like the Ancient Mariner's albatross. That failed quest—perhaps related to the failure of his earlier quest for lasting love—played out a dominant theme of his radio plays:* from failure as a biographer, he turned to triumphant success in a radio play about a nervous young biographer, Herbert Reeve, engaged on just such a quest as he had himself abandoned. Reed's hero (whose name owes something to that of Herbert Read, the poet and critic, with whom he was tired of being confused) assembles a mass of conflicting testimony about his author, the novelist Richard Shewin. His witnesses include a waspish brother, his wife, two spin-sters of uncertain virtue, and (the finest comic role he was to create for radio) the 12-tone composeress Hilda Tablet. The success of *A Very Great Man Indeed* (1953) prompted six sequels, the best of them *The Private Life of Hilda Tablet* (1954), in which Reeve is browbeaten into switching the subject of his biography from the dumb dead to the exuberantly vocal living composeress.

The modest income that Reed's work for radio brought him he supplemented with the still more modest rewards of book-reviewing and translation. The reviewing was to result in a British Council booklet, *The Novel since 1939* (1946), and his published transla-tions include Ugo Betti's *Three Plays* (1956) and *Crime on Goat Island* (1961), Balzac's *Père Goriot* (1962) and *Eugénie Grandet* (1964), and Natalia Ginzburg's *The Advertisement* (1969). Several of his translations found their way into the theatre, and in the autumn of 1955 there were London premières of no less than three. His own poems and translations of those by Leopardi continued for a time to appear, usually in the pages of the *Listener*. Douglas Cleverdon published a limited Clover Hill Edition of five *Lessons of the War* in

* See Roger Savage's excellent article, 'The Radio Plays of Henry Reed', in *British Radio Drama*, ed. John Drakakis (1981).

1970, and *The Streets of Pompeii and Other Plays for Radio* and *Hilda Tablet and Others: Four Pieces for Radio* were issued together by the BBC in 1971. In 1975 the BBC broadcast his anthology of Leopardi's poems in his own translations; a last relinquishing of work long pondered over resulted in 1974–5 in the publication of a handful of his poems in the *Listener*, with the elegiac love poem 'Bocca di Magra', perhaps written in the 1950s, as a final word. Over the years he had worked on (and seemingly completed two acts of) a three-act verse play about the false Dimitry; a long poem, called variously 'Matthew' and 'In Black and White', perhaps set during the American Civil War; a dramatic monologue, 'Clytemnestra', possibly as a pendant to his Sophoclean 'Triptych' in *A Map*; and a commissioned translation of the *Ajax* of Sophocles. He had drafted and all but finished polishing a translation of Montale's haunting *Motetti*. Reed's *Who's Who* entry for 1977 listed *The Auction Sale and Other Poems* among his publications, but no such collection ever appeared. Talk even at the end of the 1970s of a collected edition came to nothing. As a perfectionist, he could not bring himself to release what he must have recognized would be his last book until it was as good as he could make it, and it never was.

Reed greatly enjoyed his fifteen years with the BBC, his membership of the Savile Club, his London life and his frequent journeys to Italy (often on a BBC commission). But in his last decade, drink and self-neglect (his staple diet was Complan) increasingly undermined his always fragile health. His notebooks record a continuing and courageous struggle. At one point, he conducts an experiment:

> I wonder if the difficulty difficulty of writing
> could be solved by drink alone
>
> Now how much better am I writing?
>
> Now how much better am I writing? Not
> much, it seems. But oh, for freedom from
> these adventitious aids.

Again, on 10 March 1985 he notes:

After the horrors and the reliefs of the last terrible weeks I have 'resumed' what seemed like a period of hopeful convalescence (though God knows it is very painful to move about & eyesight is at rock-bottom). The Income Tax, and my all but paralysed will about it, stand in the way. Yet prowling round the three or four poems from the 50s I still want to finish occasional jerks forward do occur.

He became increasingly incapacitated and reclusive, but devoted friends never ceased to visit him in the Upper Montagu Street flat he continued to occupy, thanks to the generosity of a long-suffering landlady, until, removed to hospital, he died on 8 December 1986.

2

REED's poems of the Thirties—particularly the earlier sections of 'The Desert'—owe something of their use of the *paysage moralisé* to the landscapes of Eliot and Auden. In 'South', the traveller of 1938 hears an unexpected voice:

> 'But look more closely', the landscape suddenly told him,
>   'What do you see?'
>
> And he saw his life. He saw it, and turned away,
> And wept hot tears down the rock's hard cheek, and kissed
> Its wrinkled mouths with the kiss of passion, crying,
>   'Where is my love? . . .'

This landscape of desire is, in every sense, unsatisfactory—not least because the nature of that desire is obscured by symbolic fog.

Very different is the landscape of 1942:

> Japonica
> Glistens like coral in all of the neighbouring gardens,
>   And today we have naming of parts.

The homely word 'neighbouring' disguises the fact that this is an extension of another symbolic landscape, the archetypal landscape of desire, that garden in which Adam *named* the animals. The presence of desire is felt the more strongly here for being shown hovering at the edge of consciousness, as the speaker himself hovers at the edge of the weapon-training squad. A second difference between the two poems is that of tone—the humour that now disguises the gravity of the subject. Reed had 'studied' to good effect during his basic training in the RAOC, and would later entertain his friends with a comic imitation of a sergeant instructing his recruits. After a few performances, he noticed that the words of the weapon-training instructor, couched in the style of the military

manual, fell into certain rhythmic patterns which fascinated him
and eventually provided the structure of 'Naming of Parts'. In this
and two subsequent 'Lessons of the War', the military voice is wit-
tily counterpointed by the inner voice—more civilized and still
civilian—of a listening recruit with his mind on other matters.

Countless poems of the First World War had carried titles and/or
epigraphs in Latin. Reed followed Wilfred Owen, who in 'Dulce et
Decorum Est' had challenged and subverted that tradition, when he
chose—and emended—a Horatian epigraph for his sequence.
Horace wrote (*Odes*, 3: 26. 1–2):

> *Vixi puellis nuper idoneus*
> *Et militavi non sine gloria*

which can be roughly translated: 'Lately I've lived among girls,
creditably enough, and have soldiered not without glory.' Slyly,
Reed turns upside down the *p* of *puellis* (girls), to give *duellis*
(battles). In this way exchanging *girls* for *battles*, he cunningly
encapsulates in his epigraph the theme of the Lessons that follow.

A third difference between the two poems is the dramatic element
that in 'Naming of Parts' counterpoints the two voices. At approxi-
mately the same point in each of the first four stanzas, the recruit's
attention wanders from the instructor's lesson in the unnatural art
of handling a lethal weapon, back to the natural world: branches,
blossom, life as opposed to death. Plucked by the Army from
gardens where, at this season, he should have been enjoying the
company of his Eve, he sees the bees 'assaulting and fumbling the
flowers': the military and sexual associations of those verbs reflect-
ing the confusion in his mind. The hint of corruption, Innocence
yielding to Experience, is confirmed by the *double entendres*, the
rueful ironies, of the final stanza.

The dialectical opposition of two voices, two views of a land-
scape, is a strategy refined in two remarkable poems of Reed's
middle years. 'The Changeling' must have been written either
shortly before or shortly after his expulsion from the Eden of Gable
Court. A brilliantly condensed autobiography, it uses the changeling
figure (from his mother's fairy-stories) and the family legend of
noble descent to articulate a troubling sense of doubleness: true self
and false self. Bright landscapes darken until, as in all the best
fairy-stories,

xxv

> Love takes him by his hand,
> And the child to exile bred
> Comes to his native land.
>
> And comes, at last, to stand
> On his scented evening lawn
> Under his flowering limes,
> Where dim in the dusk and high,
> His mansion is proudly set,
> And the single light burns
> In the room where his sweet young wife
> Waits in his ancient bed.

The possessive pronoun, 'proudly set' to every item in this catalogue of Paradise Regained, begins to sound disturbingly over-insistent when extended to 'his summer sky, . . . his first pale stars'. He protests too much, masking a doubt that finally turns to desolate certainty:

> 'All this is false. And I
> Am an interloper here.'

Reed's most ambitious exploration of the landscape of desire occurs in 'The Auction Sale'. A Forsterian or Hardyesque short story, set in the Hardy country he had recently left, it is told in a voice as flat as if the speaker were reading from a country newspaper:

> Within the great grey flapping tent
> The damp crowd stood or stamped about;
> And some came in, and some went out
> To drink the moist November air . . .

After the auctioneer has rattled off the opening lots, he turns to something different, announcing '*There's a reserve upon this number.*' A shrouded object is unveiled, revealing

> The prospect of a great gold frame
> Which through the reluctant leaden air
> Flashed a mature unsullied grace
> Into the faces of the crowd.
> And there was silence in that place.

As the ordinary field of 'Judging Distances' had been succeeded by one where

> the sun and the shadows bestow
> Vestments of purple and gold[,]

in the grey tent and leaden air of the auction sale there blazes a scene as different as the language in which it is described:

> *Effulgent in the Paduan air,*
> *Ardent to yield the Venus lay*
> *Naked upon the sunwarmed earth.*

The inner voice that, in the English silence, proceeds to detail so lovingly the Italian landscape of mythologized desire can be understood to be that of the young man who now bids against the London dealers. As the figures mount, the grey voice and the golden contrapuntally compete:

> *Ardent to yield* the nods resumed
> *Venus upon the sunwarmed* nods
> *Abandoned Cupids danced* and nodded
> *His mouth towards her* bid four thousand
> Four thousand, any advance upon,
> *And still beyond* four thousand fifty
> *Unrolled towards the* nodding *sun.*

When, finally, the young man drops out of the bidding, he takes leave of his Paradise Lost with an unvoiced elegy, and is later seen—like Masaccio's Adam, but more tragic for being alone—

> in the dusk,
> Not walking on the road at all,
> But striding beneath the sodden trees . . .
> Crying. That was what she said.
> Bitterly, she later added.
> Crying bitterly, she said.

This fine poem was to prove prophetic. When in the 1970s the author of *A Map of Verona* again sought out his 'city of a long-held dream', it was too late. 'The Town Itself' is a love poem addressed to 'my darling', but Verona has other things on her mind, and the lover is unrequited:

> I shall never be accepted as a citizen:
> I am still, and shall always be, a stranger here.

Reed never abandoned his quest for the Great Good Place, and his late manuscript poems provide a poignant record of dreams and mirages encountered in the Waste Land. When he comes to 'The Château', echoes of the 23rd Psalm tell us he comes from the valley of the shadow of death. Standing outside 'the great grey mansion' ('in my father's house are many mansions'), he feels, not as the Changeling felt outside *his* mansion, that he was about to come into his own, but that his life has been going on elsewhere and otherwise:

> surely beyond that great façade my life is being lived?
> Lived, loved and filled with gaiety and ardour . . .

To reach it and take his place at 'the starry feast', he has only to cross the last threshold, a step his imagination takes with an intensity of vision that will stand comparison with the close of 'Little Gidding':*

> Surely there will be a signal? Inconspicuously,
> One of the giant roses in the gardens around us
> Will perhaps explode on to the autumn grass:
> Something like that, perhaps. I know I shall know the moment.
>
> And surely (and almost now) it will happen, and tell me
> That now I must rise and with firm footsteps tread
> Across the enormous flagstones, reach, find and know
> My own and veritable door;
> I shall open it, enter, and learn
> That in all this hungry time I have never wanted,
> But have, elsewhere, on honey and milk been fed,
> Have in green pastures somewhere lain, and in the mornings,
> Somewhere beside still waters have
> Mysteriously, ecstatically, been led.

Italy, the setting of most of the late manuscript poems, was, after Gable Court, the closest he could come to the Great Good Place on earth, but to both he comes as a stranger or 'Intruder'. The poem of that title describes his return (a charged word in Reed's lexicon) in a double capacity: an earlier self and his own 'noonday ghost', whose presence falls like a shadow between the speaker and the companion he has just embraced. The spectre is said to be seeking

* The last of Eliot's *Four Quartets* may even have been kindled in June 1941 by a spark from Reed's incendiary satire, 'Chard Whitlow', published on 10 May 1941.

> Something I dared not say,
> And bent in distress beside me
> Ashen and anguished and lonely.

What he is seeking and why a *noonday* ghost should have 'an *agèd* face' we can infer when the speaker

> ... saw he was visiting again this place
> A quarter-century hence
> And pausing and hoping and sighing,
> Recapturing a half or a third
> Of what we were saying there now,
> As though what we said had mattered,
> There by the base of the fountain
> Or at that pause on the hill-side
> Where we always said our goodbyes ...

Such goodbyes are clearly far from final, but this cunning interweaving of time past, time present, and time future ends—as a good ghost story should—with a leave-taking of another kind. After so many sunlit Italian landscapes, the wintry English cityscape of 'L'Envoi', the manuscript poem in which Reed takes leave of his reader, makes a contrast the more poignant for the genial tone of the fable's telling.

Randall Jarrell wrote that 'A good poet is someone who manages in a lifetime of standing out in thunderstorms to be struck by lightning five or six times: a dozen and he is great.' By this criterion, or any other, Henry Reed is a poet whom it is an honour to introduce as he takes his rightful place at 'the starry feast'.

from *A Map of Verona*
(1946, 1947)

PRELUDES

A MAP OF VERONA

*Quelle belle heure, quels bons bras me
rendront ces régions d'où viennent mes
sommeils et mes moindres mouvements?*

A map of Verona is open, the small strange city;
With its river running round and through, it is river-embraced,
And over this city for a whole long winter season,
Through streets on a map, my thoughts have hovered and paced.

Across the river there is a wandering suburb,
An unsolved smile on a now familiar mouth;
Some enchantments of earlier towns are about you:
Once I was drawn to Naples in the south.

Naples I know now, street and hovel and garden,
The look of the islands from the avenue,
Capri and Ischia, like approaching drum-beats—
My youthful Naples, how I remember you!

You were an early chapter, a practice in sorrow,
Your shadows fell, but were only a token of pain,
A sketch in tenderness, lust, and sudden parting,
And I shall not need to trouble with you again.

But I remember, once your map lay open,
As now Verona's, under the still lamp-light.
I thought, are these the streets to walk in in the mornings,
Are these the gardens to linger in at night?

And all was useless that I thought I learned:
Maps are of place, not time, nor can they say
The surprising height and colour of a building,
Nor where the groups of people bar the way.

3

It is strange to remember those thoughts and to try to catch
The underground whispers of music beneath the years,
The forgotten conjectures, the clouded, forgotten vision,
Which only in vanishing phrases reappears.

Again, it is strange to lead a conversation
Round to a name, to a cautious questioning
Of travellers, who talk of Juliet's tomb and fountains
And a shining smile of snowfall, late in Spring.

Their memories calm this winter of expectation,
Their talk restrains me, for I cannot flow
Like your impetuous river to embrace you;
Yet you are there, and one day I shall go.

The train will bring me perhaps in utter darkness
And drop me where you are blooming, unaware
That a stranger has entered your gates, and a new devotion
Is about to attend and haunt you everywhere.

The flutes are warm: in tomorrow's cave the music
Trembles and forms inside the musician's mind,
The lights begin, and the shifting crowds in the causeways
Are discerned through the dusk, and the rolling river behind.

And in what hour of beauty, in what good arms,
Shall I those regions and that city attain
From whence my dreams and slightest movements rise?
And what good Arms shall take them away again?

[1942]

MORNING

Look, my love, on the wall, and here, at this Eastern picture.
How still its scene, and neither of sleep nor waking:
No shadow falls from the tree or the golden mountain,
The boats on the glassy lake have no reflection,
No echo would come if you blew a horn in those valleys.

And look away, and move. Or speak, or sing:
And voices of the past murmur among your words,
Under your glance my dead selves quicken and stir,
And a thousand shadows attend you where you go.

That is your movement. There is a golden stillness,
Soundless and fathomless, and far beyond it;
When brow on brow, or mouth to mouth assembled,
We lie in the calm of morning. And there, outside us,
The sun moves on, the boat jogs on the lake,
The huntsman calls.
And we lie here, our orient peace awaking
No echo, and no shadow, and no reflection.

[1944]

5

THE RETURN

We have been off on a long voyage, have we not?
Have done and seen much in that time, but have got

Little that you will prize, who are dancing now
In the silent town whose lights gleam back from our prow.

For you we have brought no pearls or gold, you will learn,
And the best we have brought for ourselves is our glad return.

We bless the estuary lying quiet in the dark,
We praise the power that is given us to steer our barque,

With the old delight, with the sense of a brief reprieve,
Up by the snowy docks on Christmas Eve.

And though you have turned for us, and have taken your release
From us and all thought of us, yet on this night of peace

Pause for a moment, put by your dance and song:
Take to us kindly, and we shall not stay long.

We shall dock the ship, and loose the dogs to roam
And across the fallen snow shall come to our home.

The music will pause, and you will hear our knock
On the door of our home. Open. We shall not mock

Anything you may do in this sacred place.
But look for a moment, and try to recall our face,

Remember on Christmas Eve, as you stand in the doorway there
And regard us as strangers, the forgotten love we bear,

And shall bear it always over the frozen snow
When the door is shut again, and once again we go.

The souls of the forgotten, for whom there is no repose
When the music begins again, and again the doors close,

For whom a thought of yours would come the length
Of a whole dark hemisphere to give us strength.

The souls of the forgotten: others reign in our stead,
But let us go with at least your blessing on our head,

Who year after year shall creep, forgotten lover and bride,
To your door and knock, and knock, at every Christmastide,

Who, lost and ever-rejected, turn from your door and weep,
And retrace our steps to the harbour, where it lies silent and
    deep

In a slumber of snow and starlight. This is the scene we know
And shall bear in our hearts for ever as worlds away we go:

The harbour, the town, the dancing: to which the soul returns,
Lost and ever-rejected, under a Star which burns

In the zenith over the mainmast. And again it is Christmas morn,
And again in the snow and the Star's light, once again we are
    born.

[1944]

THE FOREST

Winter's white labyrinth, Poseidon's power,
    The solemn, moonless night, the coiling mist,
Could not deny, only delay, that hour,
    When we along the darkness crept and kissed.

The great ice closed upon each beast and bird,
    And we lay mute and warm in its embrace,
The soft disturbances of night we heard
    Seemed only shadows rustling to their place.

They found their place, lay quiet, and were still.
    Momentously the night reigned; phantomwise
The hours progressed upon their way; until
    There, in the glacial silence of sunrise,

We saw the ranks of serried archers stand,
Their arrows sharp and pointed, hand by hand.

[1946]

THE WALL

The place where our two gardens meet
Is undivided by a street,
And mingled flower and weed caress
And fill our double wilderness,
Among whose riot undismayed
And unreproached, we idly played,
While, unaccompanied by fears,
The months extended into years,
Till we went down one day in June
To pass the usual afternoon
And there discovered, shoulder-tall,
Rise in the wilderness a wall:
The wall which put us out of reach
And into silence split our speech.
We knew, and we had always known
That some dark, unseen hand of stone
Hovered across our days of ease,
And strummed its tunes upon the breeze.
It had not tried us overmuch,
But here it was, for us to touch.

The wilderness is still as wild,
And separately unreconciled
The tangled thickets play and sprawl
Beneath the shadows of our wall,
And the wall varies with the flowers
And has its seasons and its hours.
Look at its features wintrily
Frozen to transparency;
Through it an icy music swells
And a brittle, brilliant chime of bells:
Would you conjecture that, in Spring,
We lean upon it, talk and sing,
Or climb upon it, and play chess
Upon its summer silentness?
One certain thing alone we know:
Silence or song, it does not go.

A habit now to wake with day
And watch it catch the sun's first ray,
Or terrorized, to scramble through
The depths of night to prove it true.

We need not doubt, for such a wall
Is based in death, and does not fall.

[1943]

OUTSIDE AND IN

Suddenly I knew that you were outside the house.
The trees went silent you were prowling among,
The twig gave warning, snapped in the evening air,
And all the birds in the garden finished singing.
What have you come for? Have you come in peace?
Or have you come to blackmail, or just to know?

And after sunset must I be made to watch
The lawn and the lane, from the bed drawn to the window,
The winking glass on top of the garden wall,
The shadows relaxing and stiffening under the moon?
I am alone, but look, I have opened the doors,
And the house is filling with cold, the winds flow in.

A house so vulnerable and divided, with
A mutiny already inside its walls,
Cannot withstand a siege. I have opened the doors
In sign of surrender. The house is filling with cold.
Why will you stay out there? I am ready to answer.
The doors are open. Why will you not come in?

[1939]

THE DOOR AND THE WINDOW

My love, you are timely come, let me lie by your heart.
For waking in the dark this morning, I woke to that mystery,
Which we can all wake to, at some dark time or another:
Waking to find the room not as I thought it was,
But the window further away, and the door in another direction.

This was not home, and you were far away,
And I woke sick, and held by another passion,
In the icy grip of a dead, tormenting flame,
Consumed by the night, watched by the door and the window,
On a bed of stone, waiting for the day to bring you.

The window is sunlit now, the spring day sparkles beyond it,
The door has opened: and can you, at last beside me,
Drive under the day that frozen and faithless darkness,
With its unseen torments flickering, which neither
The dearest look nor the longest kiss assuages?

[1944]

HIDING BENEATH THE FURZE

(Autumn 1939)

Hiding beneath the furze as they passed him by,
   He drowned their talk with the noise of his own heart,
And faltering, came at last to the short hot road
   With the flat white cottage under the rowan trees:
And this can never happen, ever again.

Before his fever drowned him, he stumbled in,
   And the old woman rose, and said in the dialect, 'Enter'.
He entered, and drank, and hearing his fever roaring,
   Surrendered himself to its sweating luxuries:
And this can never happen, ever again.

There were bowls of milk, and (after such hunger) bread.
   Here was the night he had longed for on the highway.
Strange, that his horror could dance so gaily in sunlight,
   And rescue and peace be here in the smoky dark:
And this can never happen, ever again.

When he awoke, he found his pursuers had been,
   But the woman had lied, and easily deceived them.
She had never questioned his right—for who so childish
   Could ever do wrong? 'He is my son', she had said:
And this can never happen, ever again.

The days passed into weeks, and the newspapers came,
   And he saw that the world was safe, and his name
      unmentioned.
He could return to the towns and his waiting friends,
   The evil captain had fled defeated to Norway:
And this can never happen, ever again.

And this can never happen, ever again.
   He stands on the icy pier and waits to depart,
The town behind him is lightless, his friends are dead,
   The captain will set his spies in his very heart,
And the fever is gone that rocked inside his head.

LIVES

You cannot cage a field.
You cannot wire it, as you wire a summer's roses
To sell in towns; you cannot cage it
Or kill it utterly. All you can do is to force
Year after year from the stream to the cold woods
The heavy glitter of wheat, till its body tires
And the yield grows weaker and dies. But the field never dies,
Though you build on it, burn it black, or domicile
A thousand prisoners upon its empty features.
You cannot kill a field. A field will reach
Right under the streams to touch the limbs of its brothers.

But you can cage the woods.
You can throw up fences, as round a recalcitrant heart
Spring up remonstrances. You can always cage the woods,
Hold them completely. Confine them to hill or valley,
You can alter their face, their shape; uprooting their outer
    saplings
You can even alter their wants, and their smallest longings
Press to your own desires. The woods succumb
To the paths made through their life, withdraw the trees,
Betake themselves where you tell them, and acquiesce.
The woods retreat; their protest of leaves whirls
Pitifully to the cooling heavens, like dead or dying prayers.

But what can you do with a stream?
You can widen it here, or deepen it there, but even
If you alter its course entirely it gives the impression
That this is what it always wanted. Moorhens return
To nest or hide in the reeds which quickly grow up there,
The fishes breed in it, stone settles on to stone.
The stream announces its places where the water will bubble
Daily and unconcerned, contentedly ruffling and scuffling
With the drifting sky or the leaf. Whatever you do,
A stream has rights, for a stream is always water;
To cross it you have to bridge it; and it will not flow uphill.

CHARD WHITLOW

(*Mr Eliot's Sunday Evening Postscript*)

As we get older we do not get any younger.
Seasons return, and today I am fifty-five,
And this time last year I was fifty-four,
And this time next year I shall be sixty-two.
And I cannot say I should care (to speak for myself)
To see my time over again—if you can call it time,
Fidgeting uneasily under a draughty stair,
Or counting sleepless nights in the crowded Tube.

There are certain precautions—though none of them very
    reliable—
Against the blast from bombs, or the flying splinter,
But not against the blast from Heaven, *vento dei venti*,
The wind within a wind, unable to speak for wind;
And the frigid burnings of purgatory will not be touched
By any emollient.
               I think you will find this put,
Far better than I could ever hope to express it,
In the words of Kharma: 'It is, we believe,
Idle to hope that the simple stirrup-pump
Can extinguish hell.'

             Oh, listeners,
And you especially who have switched off the wireless,
And sit in Stoke or Basingstoke, listening appreciatively to the
    silence
(Which is also the silence of hell), pray not for yourselves but
    your souls.

And pray for me also under the draughty stair.
As we get older we do not get any younger.

And pray for Kharma under the holy mountain.

                            [1941]

THE DESERT

I SAILORS' HARBOUR

My thoughts, like sailors becalmed in Cape Town harbour,
Await your return, like a favourable wind, or like ˙
New tackle for the voyage, without which it is useless starting.
We watch the sea daily, finish our daily tasks
By ten in the morning, and with the day to waste,
Wander through the suburbs, with quiet thoughts of the brothels,
And sometimes thoughts of the churches.

In the eating-houses we always contrive to get near to
The window, where we can keep an eye on the life-
Bearing sea. Suddenly a wind might blow, and we must not miss
First sight of the waves as they darken with promise for us.
We have been here too long. We know the quays,
And the streets near the quays, more than should ever be
    necessary.
When can we go on our way?

Certain we are of this, that when the wind comes,
It may be deceptive and sweet and finally blow
To shipwreck and ruin between here and the next port of call.
At all times we think of this. At last we have come to know
The marine charts can safely assure us of less and less
As we go farther south. So we cannot go out on the boulevards
Or climb Table Mountain.

Though if we had certainty, here there might be delight.
But all that is world in itself, the mountain, the streets,
The sand-dunes outside the town, we shyly and sadly return
    from.
They are too much to bear. And our curiosity
Lies alone in the over-scrubbed decks and the polished brasses
(For we have to look trim in the port) and in
The high-piled ambiguous cargo.

[1938]

16

II THE CAPTAIN

It was shipwreck, after all.
The sides burst in, and the masts
Broke, and one huge white sail
Flowed beautiful over the sea,
Till the suck drew it under.

He saw then at last that he
Had not for himself alone
Made punishment. As they split,
He thought, 'Oh God, how man
Makes his own thunder'.

He had known all along that this
Would happen. And great remorse
Filled him as he saw his men
Swimming to the dreadful mouths
Of the sharks for plunder.

[1937]

III SOUTH

They had seen for a hundred days their shadows on ice.
What suffering god whose image they were made in
Had drawn them curious to his blizzard centre,
      And sent them back?

Who knew? Unanswered, they returned unspeaking
To the brutal coast their dreams had kept familiar,
And came in the last few hours to where a rock
      Rose from the ice.

Careful but unreflectingly, they passed across it,
And went their way, save one. He on the rock
Pressed suddenly against the rock for comfort,
      And comfort came.

(Rocks were so rare, one should not pass them by.)
After a time he opened his eyes. Yes, thinking,
'The others? I cannot stay here on a rock for ever',
      He opened his eyes,

And there was a world. He had curved his arms right over
His head, and his cheek pressed hard against the rock,
And all he saw was his fragment of rock, and beyond it,
      A fraction of sea.

He saw at once it was strange. For so many days,
There had been no place where he might not see the ice,
And the blossoming of ice and snow under visible winds
      From the mountain-range,

Till an ignorant gesture had hidden them utterly.
He watched. The world remained. And the silent bay
And the great black rock passed through his waiting veins
      The shock of peace.

It might be a bay, he thought, on the summer islands,
Far in the north. (North? They had once been south.)
'But look more closely', the landscape suddenly told him,
      'What do you see?'

18

And he saw his life. He saw it, and turned away,
And wept hot tears down the rock's hard cheek, and kissed
Its wrinkled mouths with the kiss of passion, crying,
  'Where is my love?

'Now? At this moment?' The world broke at his words.
In the little prison the furious prisoner howling
Showed him through glaciers the heart's still unforgotten
  Knocking of blood.

And showed him too that there would be no return.
His coasts henceforth would calve in change unceasing,
And like a ship, the heart would shake and tack
  To a varying port,

Beneath whose recondite stars another quiet,
Not peace but like it, awaited him now, and held
Its tortured arms of truth to receive its lovers:
  It was the ice.

'Ice will come drifting over our sighs like music,
Now and forever', he whispered, 'And though from sleep,
We wake up weeping, our tears we shall find are frozen,
  As soon as wept.

'And of that we must learn to be glad. Goodbye', he cried.
'Oh delusive rock, we shall not come here again',
And climbing round and down and after the others,
  Faced the full day.

            [1938]

IV THE BUILDERS

Explorers have come to the places a few years after
And have found the villages sunken from sight and the river
Covering the unfinished landing-stages, and nothing besides.

Us too and our days completely the years shall cover,
But what rediscoverer save me shall come curiously
To plot by the stars and the sun the exact positions

Where we built, where we made our plans in the ramshackle
  office
Where we prepared so keenly and laughed so loudly
At the details of civilization we should import

There in the jungle. We were not inexperienced; no,
We knew the life would be strenuous, we were careful
Our plans should not be irrevocable; we would not remove

Too suddenly the barbarous and broken relics about us,
Where others had worshipped and loved; we saw too plainly
Why they had failed and why their temples fell.

But we knew they had been excellent in heart like us,
Only over-ambitious; had tried in their folly to bring
The world at the very start to watch their successes,

Their splendid creations under their splendid sky.
No, we would build and trade in a moderate way
With the passing canoe-men who went up and down the river.

And so we began to tug from the reluctant earth
Her overgrowth and her foulness; avoiding the clouds,
The disastrous heat of the noons and the random storms.

Till that storm came which we were forced to watch
Slowly and cruelly havocking a whole day's work.
And one of us turned, and forgot what we both had come for.

Ah, what discoverer will think to discover this?
By the river's edge, after the storm had gone,
Who will record how one of us said to the other,

'The plans have been false ones. There is an error, I know it.
What is this storm that comes, in season and out,
And is not us, but destroys us? I have tried so hard

'To find the mistake, thinking it might be something,
Though unforeseen, that we yet could combat together.
But it seems it is something else: you know how it is.

'I have felt for some days that I ought to tell you of this.
(I was being unfair to us both.) And now I am going,
But I do not go in enmity. Remember that.'

He remembered that. Remembered it in his walks,
Daily, alone in their thoughtful, single street,
Remembered plainly the melody of their two voices,

Question and answer, till the winds and the rotting rains
Swept the months forward, choking and filling the gaps
Like an orchestration. 'In enmity. Remember that.'

Till every corner and every excavation
Had the clear new meaning of an emended text,
And the ditches they had dug seemed filled with dead.

This, this, oh how should they know, who will only have heard
That his observations are not to be relied on,
That he finished as best he could certain tasks of science

But the best was not good? There are rumours along the river
Of his ingratitude to the pilot and oarsmen
Who took him the thousand miles to the estuary:

'It is said he was brutal to one of the carefree natives
Who laughed at the unfinished buildings, calling them ruins,
As they stood in the slender boat and watched them retreat.

And every summer the river, rising and falling,
Has claimed as its own some grotesque, pathetic memorial,
Irresponsibly hugging and kissing and sucking it outwards.

What marks in time have we made? 'None, none,' they will
   answer,
'All we could find was the space in the forest and only
The cross on the temple, islanded above the waters.'

[1939]

V THE PLACE AND THE PERSON

The place not worth describing, but like every empty place.
So much like other empty places, you yourself
Must paint its picture, who have your own such places,
Which lie, their whitening eyes turned upwards to the sky,
On the remoter side of a continent,
Under a burning sun. Their streets and hovels
Have lost all memory, and their harbours rot.
Paint it, and vary it as you like, but only
Always paint this: the solitary figure,
Who lies or squats or sits, facing the sun,
Now in bewilderment or a vacant calm,
In filthy rags, the ancient garb of exiles,
The casual mixture of others' memories,
Legacy or theft; and the mind perplexed and eroded.
In such a one, at the edge of his world, desire
Is buried or burned in lust, and love is banished
Beyond the creeping jungle; in the noontime heat,
Since even these can be lost, they are far away.
You will know all this, and can paint it as suits you best,
But paint alone the central figure faithfully;
His surroundings do not matter: they are yours or mine,
The walls perhaps with greying notices
Of the bygone sales of heifers, or the concourse
Of a troupe of vanished singers, singing there,
The carrion birds shuffling upon the roof,
The empty expanse of ocean confronting him,
The harbour steps, the empty sands below,
And the movement of water on the harbour bar.
And from the emptiness, still mute but moving,
Emerge the dancers who will not be still.
Nearest at hand two scuffling figures, who
Saunter a little and scuffle again and dance,
Or lie on the paving-stones and yawn at each other,
A daily ritual; if not with them, with others.
This is a dance, with ritual and celebration.
Others join in its windings as the day
Passes through noon and afternoon and evening
And wave on wave of heat and sunlight fall,

Illuminating and transfixing, and at last
The dreadful pattern of their lives disclosing.
From out of rocks and paths they come, the dancers:
One who walks solitary and shuns the gaze
Of the scuffling pair, now languid in the heat,
Until, withdrawn, he looks about and secretly
Seizing a dead shark's jawbone out of air,
Makes it a trap with stones and vegetation
For yet another who walks on the level beaches.
They congregate, beseeching or resentful,
Till the empty place is crowded with silent ghosts.
They are intangible, but he is one with them,
As with their proud, vindictive admonitions,
And sensual taunts, and gestures of possession,
They separate, part, return, link arms again,
Familiarly, yet not with reconcilement.
And, one with them, he cannot turn away,
Or forget in the motions of song and prayer and dance
The great dried fountains of their sombre eyes.

They are here and not here, sometimes all of them here,
And sometimes only an insistent couple,
Who do not go away, but repeat their figure,
And sing again and again their wordless song,
And pray their speechless prayer. The hours pass,
And it is still high noon; they are here and not here,
And a voice without speaking murmurs into the air:
'You have prayed too much, and in mid-prayer have known it
And faltered there. You have sung too much,
And the song has travelled an echoing wall and returned;
Have danced too much and in the entwining figures
Have faltered there; and have too often chosen
The rituals of despair and joy, and faltered.
Have danced, prayed, sung: but have not wept enough.'

All yields. The wooden buildings by the shore
Split in the heat. The blackened sand
Cracks into arid chasms and fissures, crumbles,
The vegetation shrivels, seeds from the chattering pod
Fall in the dust. But the untouchable stone

24

Which cannot weep, refracts the light and glitters
And cannot turn or yield, but suffers and endures.
Weeping and yielding, they are far away,
The sun and the man in close encounter stand
And neither conquers. Only a burst of rain
Could fall between them, make these burning stones
Places for hands and feet; only a wind
Fall and unlock their embrace. And so he mutters:
'Give me a wind; or give me a burst of rain.
The sun will not yield, being unconquerable,
And how can I yield, who wander and only find
No one to whom defeat may be confessed?'

His own words lure him: and 'Alas,' he murmurs:
'What do these comings and goings profit me,
Pains and adventures among foreign races,
The languages I cram my brain with, and
The ills unspeakable? What shall I do with these
If after many years they do not lead me
One day to rest in a place where I may say
This pleases me, and here I may remain?
What do these comings and goings profit me,
These instruments I finger and re-learn,
These books whose pages blind me in the sun,
And, worse than all, the howling conversations
Which without cease construct themselves within me,
Disposing guilt for every suffered pain,
On all my journeys wheresoever I go;
And what are foreign tongues for, but to choke
My mouth with references to former travellers,
Who have not gone this way, or such ways, long before?'

There is no reply; the dancers for once have chosen
To withdraw themselves, and the beaches are really bare.
And beyond the beaches the other vision rises
Which is their counterpart and their negation.
From the far horizon, and breaking in triumph towards him,
A ship comes forth, with supernatural haste
Parting the waters; and with grace the waves
Draw from her painted sides. Seductively

She flourishes her dazzling burden of sails
Which without wind or tide approach the harbour.
He sees her, and rises and cries, 'Again, again!
This ship will go tomorrow, and I shall go with it!'
And to the empty hovels he turns, but the dancers
Do not emerge, and their movements cannot be heard.
He calls to them: 'This ship will go tomorrow.
And if I am in your debt, to whatever degree,
Tell me at once, for I depart tomorrow.
I shall not wait for the unreturning vessels
Of you who dance your dances on this shore.
This is my ship; its name I do not know.
And since, if you ask the first dog in the street,
It will know enough to tell you I am helpless,
An impotent and wretched, and can do little or nothing,
And least of all for myself, do me this final act,
Who have never done me anything so gentle:
Find me the time of this golden ship's departure,
For, paralysed, I wish most earnestly to get
Early on board. Find me and tell me when.'

The ship draws closer, triumphant and unconcerned,
Unpiloted, and with the deliverer's smile,
And confidently cargoed with a love
That has broken through virgin seas to seek and find him,
Wherefore it gleams more brightly, wherefore it glitters.
The ropes are quickly thrown to where the harbour
Gladly receives them; the gang-planks quickly descend
And women in green and purple come from the deck
Descend to the jetty, bearing a burden of oil,
And some with flowers, and all of these they dispose
Close to his feet, and withdraw. The ship fills the harbour,
And to the ship they return. It gleams more brightly,
And its gleam is the gleam of yet another deception.
For look, the sails, their powerful and striding canvas,
And the riding fortress of timber which is the hull,
Are changing there in the sunlight, undone and mastered
As all is undone and mastered that comes this way;
Dislimning, falling, dissolving, canvas to satin,
Satin to sunlight turning, wood to paper,

The masts to cobwebs, women to wraith and phantom,
Failing mirage of the noontime, sunlight to sea,
Cobweb and satin to sunlight, sunlight to sun,
The empty harbour an unattended altar
For the barren, unblest marriage of sun and sea.

Fed on such visions, how shall a man recover
Between the dancing dream and the dream of departure?
For the dancers go, and their silent song and prayer
Go with them; and the ship goes from the harbour,
Vanishes in sea, or drowns in air, but goes.
The waves of noon can barely reach the shore,
And the jungle approaches always a little nearer.
This is the captive. And paint him as you will.
These are my images. The place not worth describing.

[1945]

Whatever sort of garden
You, I, or we shall build,
Neglected much, or cared for,
And all its great designs
Fulfilled or unfulfilled:
Built over ruined shrines,
Where others have loved and worshipped,
Or built on virgin ground:
Shaped or disorderly,
Let it at least be
Different from this:

From the hot, eternal tropic's
Thick, flamboyant flower,
The senseless blazing heat
Creeping through minute and hour:
Let it suffer autumn and spring,
Its trees deciduous,
Let it flower in sudden moments
For you, me, or us:
Whatever its weathers bring,
Let it at least not lie
Under the burning kiss
Of eternal summer sky.

And whether it stand
With its precincts walled or open,
Or whether a city surround it,
Or it stand at the sea's edge,
With the wild and the broken beyond it,
Where the winds flicker and hiss,
Let it at least have this:
Among its ruined temples,
Let there be certain ways
Wherein, darkness or day,
You, I, or we
Finally, certainly, may,
Skirting the shattered fragments,
Wander and praise.

[1945]

TINTAGEL

I TRISTRAM

Tristram's tower
Rises and falls and rises.

The ruin leads your thoughts
Past the moments of darkness when silence fell over the hall,
And the only sound rising was the sound of frightened breathing,
Past the lies and pursuits, the arraignments and accusations,
To the perpetually recurring story,
The doorway open, either in the soft green weather,
The gulls seen over the purple-threaded sea, the cliffs,
Or open in mist,
The gulls heard over and under you in the greyness—
This time or that, but always the doorway open,
And through the broken stones the forbidden courtyard,
And under the archway, ever, ever,
Bold in clear weather or halting through the mist,
The eternal reappearance of Iseult.

Tristram's tower
Rises and falls and rises.
It is often rebuilt completely, or its ruins
Are draped with cultivated vegetation. Or we try
To preserve in it the character of a day
Seized somewhere from the past, a resting-place,
An intermediate moment of decline.
Sometimes it comes unsummoned as if by magic.
And sometimes when we could best prevent, we let it
Form and rebuild itself before our eyes.
For some, at each return it comes more faintly,
Less echoing, and more than ever sterile,
A deeper draught of the potion asked each time,
Each time more salt the flowers in the walls,
Wider each time the vision through the window
Where the sea leaps waste and empty.

29

And few have either the power or the resolution
To unbuild it stone by stone,
We cannot learn to forget as sometimes we learn to remember,
To compose an oblivion like a memory,
To capture carefully an empty future,
As we recapture, fragment by fragment, the past.

We build the ruin, or the ruin appears for us,
We are forced to the windows, or we ask an attendant to watch,
At the earliest lift of dawn, the sails appearing,
To break the news as gently as possible to us,
If the sails are white or black.

And under the gulls the mounting and falling sea
Chatters and roars and groans throughout the night
Against the unyielding cliff where Tristram's tower
Rises and falls and rises.

II ISEULT BLAUNCHESMAINS

There are also those who watch the land from the sea,
Tapping a foot resignedly upon the boat-deck,
Who have followed their loves to the harbourage of their lands
And may not enter.

'And if you follow them to their land, you find it
As they have said, but smaller, and you know it
Only as a land you will not set foot upon.
Cornwall is much like Brittany, they have told you,
But the cliffs stand up in foreignness about you
And shout their echoes which you cannot catch,
And the sea explodes on the rocks in a different language.'

It is thus we can hear her, speaking at the end of her journey
And the beginning of her return: Iseult Blaunchesmains,
Looking upon a coast and a foreign castle,
And valleys not hostile, but their hillsides
Turning themselves indifferently away;
Or seawards where the sun breaks through and raises
Voluptuous isles of sunlight from the water.

'Bright as the day may be, sunlit the water,
I am caught in that ellipse, that dark tumultuous eye,
Where one black circle, expanding over water,
Crosses another. This tale has existed before:
In the golden collapse of the summer, or the tearing days
Before the beginning of spring, remembered weathers
Which they will always forget, they come with their griefs,
They come with their years around them in a leaden circle,
Fatigued and baffled with the stress of understanding.
They rest in you: in you their story grows
Until you find, as another season enters,
Their story becoming yours, at first a part of your story,
And then your story wholly.

'They have entered your lands,
And you think you may enter theirs.

'But you are not their story, you are only
A season of ease and of recuperation,
At most a beguiling and mistaken footpath,
A hidden brake in the maze of a burning forest
Where the defeated creature may hide and recover.
And that day comes when they retrace their steps
Through the burnt-out wood, where round the blackened stumps
The fresh green flickers and waves; or back once more
Along the diverging footpath taking their way,
Over a hill or a sea.

'They leave your land, your now half-empty story,
And following, following, across the empty sea,
You hurry with your questions towards their harbours.
And there you come to the castle, small in its ruins,
Or splendid with its reviving banners flying,
But never yours, and never to be known by you.

'The sea explodes on the rocks in a different language,
And only yours is the wind blown off the valleys,
The answering wind, the land-wind, wind of departure.'

[1943]

III KING MARK

Dismount: let the horns grow faint in the distance.
Leave them behind, and climb alone with your purpose
Over curving slopes, stumbling in hidden water-courses,
Where the brambles clutch at your feet, or the grass grows over,
And the sharp rocks offer you their sudden surprises,
Some alchemy of the light, on such a day,
Bends on us, presses us,
Across the golden growth of frond and leaf
So that today
The heart is led in submission, spelled by the heat,
By the sunflower's weather, while the flower turns to the sun,
To seek out its own doom, without postponement.

Follow the narrow ways, the overgrown tracks,
Disturbing the hidden creatures. Cross and ignore
The fair wide road,
Lonely but good for traffic,
And now in summer by the idle froth
Of verdure so caressingly invaded.

Somewhere beyond, and held in a dream of summer,
Lies the familiar place, familiar,
And desperately unknown. And high or low,
Under that sky, through every branch and bracken,
In every fibre of the sunflower-hedge, in every ripple
Of air among the grasses, silent glint
Of light on leaf, the sense of prearrangement,
And the sense of a new death. Forever and forever,
This place has waited for you, created leaf and flower,
Twisted the tree and the branch to their proper pattern,
Has shaped the stream in its course for you to remember,
Forever waiting. And may wait, again and again.
Go through the sunflower-hedge.
The collapsing slide of a castle beneath the waves
Is not more absolute. There they lay
And the sword lay naked between them.
A roar of resurgent waters cries over the ruins,
And over the whirlpool the white gulls falter and mount,

And the sounds of lament come from them. Never had she
  seemed
More blest, nor more of a blessing. Under shallow water
The tower is a treacherous and eternal rock. And the day
Never had seemed more empty. Murmur of stream and insect,
Dazzle of sun and flower. Oh, turn, turn, turn
A face to the sun, or a weeping face to the wall.
There are many ways of answering.

                                And some cry bitterly,
And some with anger blindly darken the light,
And some press to their lips a golden lie
That this is innocence, the pair with a sword between them.
But to King Mark, who counted on all of these ways,
The heat of the summer stirred and whispered, 'Go:
Cover the scene from view, dissemble your intrusion,
You have played your part in it: *concurritur*.
Pull back the flowers with their harsh great stalks,
Kick from the grass the mark and track of your footsteps.
Neither he nor she is yours. You are no sword,
Nor any sword can part them. Return through the flames
And the fires of summer, where the green invades
The fair wide road,
Lonely but good for traffic: cross and ignore.
You have fallen upon a grotto of sudden light
And it is so bright you cannot call it darkness.'

[1945]

34

IV ISEULT LA BELLE

Bold in clear weather, or halting through the mist,
I have seen it all, and shall see it again and again:
The taut strained body of Tristram climbing the rocks,
The sunlit fear of Mark in the magic grotto,
The desolate parted lips of that other Iseult
Lost to the language of this dangerous coast.
I am she, the heart and centre of desire,
The well-beloved, the eternally-reappearing
Ghost on the lips of spring.

            And do you expect a face
Calm at the heart of torment? Calmness in me, the fear
Of all the poets who dreaded the passing of beauty,
And called on Time to stay his decaying hand,
And who, in their hearts, dreaded more than beauty's passing,
Its perpetual arrest?

            I am that point of arrest;
Though I drop back into oblivion, though I retreat
Into the soft, hoarse chant of the past, the unsoaring, dull
And songless harmony behind the screen of stone,
I do not age.
But I come, in whatever season, like a new year,
In such a vision as the open gates reveal
As you saunter into a courtyard, or enter a city,
And inside the city you carry another city,
Inside delight, delight.
And it seems you have borne me always, the love within you,
Under the ice of winter, hidden in darkness.
Winter on winter, frozen and unrevealing,
To flower in a sudden moment, the bloom held high towards
    heaven,
Steady in the glowing air the white and gleaming calyx.
Lightness of heart.

            So, I am hard to remember,
As summer is hard to remember in the press of winter,
When the waking kiss is a snowflake on the mouth,

The petals lost and forgotten; and, as you move to embrace me,
I am that weary face, that fearful rejecting hand,
Which begs for freedom from you.
And under the dark the waves groan again on the rocks,
The hungry ruins divide the mists among them,
The land-wind and sea-wind meeting.

                        Do you expect a heart,
Unmoved, and tears unfallen? Oh, look again:
Am I not yourself as well?
And do I not know the arena of separation,
Encircled and watched by the indifferent fields of corn,
The heavy fountains of trees in the shining heat,
The hillsides and rivers, grasses and level beaches;
Even so close you may touch them with your hand,
They are inaccessible; yet they burn the sense.

And do you think I would not reach towards you,
As the screen of stone falls into place between us,
And the dirge begins, do you think I do not know
That somewhere beyond me, lost, and lost and falling,
(Do you think I do not know?)
That under the droning gales which tear the stones,
When you dare not move a step in the dark which surrounds
    you,
You strive to find some angle of the broken castle,
And tug at the streaming earth to find some spot
In which you may plant your torn chimerical flowers
With a ruined wall to protect them?

O you, who will never be other than children,
Do you think, if I could, I would not reach my hand,
Through the burning mist and the echoing night of blackness,
To bless you, soothe you, and guide you through your hell?

[1945]

36

TRIPTYCH

CHRYSOTHEMIS

I cannot follow them into their world of death,
Or their hunted world of life, though through the house,
Death and the hunted bird sing at every nightfall.
I am Chrysothemis: I sailed with dipping sails,
Suffered the winds I would not strive against,
Entered the whirlpools and was flung outside them,
Survived the murders, triumphs and revenges.
Survived; and remain in a falling, decaying mansion,
A house detested and dark in the setting sun,
The furniture covered with sheets, the gardens empty,
A brother and sister long departed,
A railing mother gone.
It is my house now. I have set myself to protect,
Against the demons that linger inside our walls,
Their saddened, quiet children of darkness and shame:
They lie on inherited beds in their heavy slumbers,
Their faces relaxed to nocturnal innocence.
I will protect them in the decaying palace.

In the dying sun, through slots in the shuttered windows,
I can see the hanging gardens carved on our mountain
Above and below us, terraces, groves and arbours,
The careful rise of the trees to meet the heavens,
The deliberate riot of the wilderness,
The silent arch through which my brother returned,
And again returned.

In the long broad days of summer,
On the great hill the house lay, lost and absorbed and dreaming,
The gardens glittered under the sweeping sun,
The inmates kept to their rooms, and hope
Rose in the silence.

                    And indeed
It seemed the agony must die. But then
The house would seem to sigh, and then again,

A sigh and another silence. Through the slotted shutters
I would see them there, my mother and my sister
Wandering and meeting in the garden's quiet
(And I moved from room to room to see them better).
There seemed a truce between them, as if they had
Called off their troops in order to bury their dead.
I could not hear my sister speak; but clearly,
She spoke with calm and patience, and my mother gave
The answer designed to please, wistful and eager;
And her words would be quietly taken, twisted and turned,
Ropes, that would loose the rivers to flood again;
The fragile dams would burst, indeed constructed
Only for breaking down.

This was the yawn of time while a murder
Awaited another murder. I did not see
My father's murder, but I see it now always around me,
And I see it shapeless: as when we are sometimes told
Of the heroes who walk out into the snow and blizzard
To spare their comrades' care, we always see
A white direction in which the figure goes,
And a vague ravine in which he stumbles and falls.
My father rises thus from a bath of blood,
Groping from table to chair in a dusky room
Through doorways into darkening corridors,
Falling at last in the howling vestibule.

In the years that followed, the winds of time swept round
The anniversaries of the act; and they
Were shouted down: my mother prepared for them
Music and dance, and called them celebrations.
They did not, fever-laden, creep on her unaware.
But did the nights not turn on her? Did she not
Dream music in the false-dawn faltering, phrases
Repeating endlessly, a figure of the dance
Halting and beckoning?

It is my house now, decaying but never dying,
The soul's museum, preserving and embalming
The shuttered rooms, the amulets, the pictures,

The doorways waiting for perennial surprises,
The children sleeping under the heat of summer,
And lastly the great bronze doors of the bridal chamber,
Huge and unspeaking, not to be pressed and opened,
Not to be lingered near, then or thereafter,
Not to be pounded upon by desolate fists,
Mine least of all.

                    I sailed with dipping sails.
I was not guilty of anybody's blood.
I will protect them in the decaying house.

With this resolve, concluded like a prayer,
From the eyes of the window gently stealing away,
As in a ritual I wipe the dust from the mirror
And look through the dark at the dim reflection before me.
The lips draw back from the mouth,
The night draws back from the years,
And there is the family smile in the quivering room.

The sun has gone, and the hunted bird demands:
'*Can the liar guard the truth, the deceiver seek it,*
The murderer preserve, the harlot chasten, or the guilty
Shelter the innocent? And shall you protect?'

[1943]

ANTIGONE

—I am come, like you. I was one of today's onlookers,
And drawn from the dark by a flicker of love and pity
I return again to the spot, to see the foot-prints
Which the dust of the market-place preserves and holds,
Before the wind and the dark shall wipe them out.
The pillars still are hot from the heat of day,
Returning the air its warmth; and here between them,
Antigone, child of the blind old man,
Stood, who will cast her shadow on earth no longer.
The dark, and the dying evening, murmur within me,
The pulse in my head, the drums in the outer suburbs,
And if I defy for this brief moment the curfew,
It is not that courage has risen, but that fear has failed for a
    moment.

—Where have you come from?

—I have forgotten. It seems
I have slipped out somehow into the summer night
From a hovel of piety, whose earthen floors
Are whispered across by trembling ghosts of passion
Which I suppress or evade. And where I once found only
Familiar unchanging quiet, now I find
Waves of a deeper silence, crossed and blown
By a wind on sentry-go, and a disturbance
Breathed through the city and lurking in the door-ways,
And though I return to the same place, can I ever
Return in the same way, can it ever be the same
Now that I see the forms of piety broken
In a minute of greater piety?

—What was the act you saw?

—I could have told you today,
But tonight I am not so certain. It is not that an act
    accomplished
Alters so soon. Perhaps it has not altered.
Perhaps it is still the act the state denounced,

Outrageous perhaps, but merely one act of defiance
Which might have been any other that we can think of.
A page of history half understood:
The act of a sister who put the love of a brother
Before the laws of a country and the world's promise:
The shaken handfuls of dust that fell and saved him
From the quick quiet hands of the thief and the deliberate
Jaws of the vulture. And thus her action
May be remembered by those who never saw her.
But an act may grow while still it remains the same.
Help me to hold it! I am of those who wander
Until death shrugs us casually away.
At most I see
On cheeks of others the tears I dread to weep.
She is of those who take and force the cup
Between the lips of the reluctant and the dying;
Who raise for a moment the disturbing wind
Through the gates of iron and stone.
And after they pass,
Having shaken a city, or broken the curse on a family,
The city's curfew blows, the family
Collect the fragments of their ruined secrets
To hide from each other's glance. And she proceeds
On into death, amazed at the world's amazement,
And the world cannot shake her with guilt, for she has achieved
Innocence again.

—And what of the world she leaves?

—I am that world, oh listen.
A drooping wind has been set to sigh on the silence
And disappear into darkness; there is a pause
Of waiting till it sighs again and goes.
Little and weary, it weighs on the brain and heart
The burdens that the soul has never borne
And has refused to bear. That is the world's
Hour and its day. That is the time I pass.
But at the day's centre, a light on its babbling shore,
Glitters the minute when the wind and the darkness lift:

'I am cast,' she said, 'for the part of love not of hatred.'
The bubble of silence at the core of the roaring tumult.

In the press of the years with the wind wreathing about us,
As we stumble our way to the faith that best supports us
Or the faith we best can bear; as we drift with the wind
Or falter and pause in the dark, there will be moments
When she returns. The greyness itself will wane,
And through the mist the glaring scene be set:
Creon again on the throne, the court-house crowded
Again with the white strained faces; Haimon
Will plead and be lost again, Ismene will turn away
In a trail of helpless tears. Again the neglected corpse
Outside the city walls will lie and be lonely.

And she is here, between these stones still breathing,
At the minute of her farewell, her withdrawing glance of
    amazement
For the world that rejects her; and the minute extends
While you stand at gaze and the centuries rise and fall.

Small and remote, between these rocks she speaks,
And her affirming whisper crosses the stones.

[1947]

42

PHILOCTETES

I have changed my mind; or my mind is changed in me.
A shadow lifts, a light comes down, the agony
Of years ceases, the blind eyes open, and the blinded body
Feels the sensation of a god descending,
A shudder of wind through the caves, the shiver of the dawn-
     wind crossing,
The wind which pauses a moment, to bless and caress and kiss
The waters pausing between the last slow wave of night,
And the first slow wave of morning.
It is a god that clasps and releases me thus. Day breaks,
And draws me up from the deepest well of night,
Where I am all and nothing, never and forever,
And sets me brimming on the lip of day, wherein
I am but Philoctetes, at only one point in a story.

On such a day in summer, before a temple,
The wound first broke and bled.
To my companions become unbearable,
I was put on this island. But the story
As you have heard it is with time distorted,
And passion and pity have done their best for it.
They could only report as they saw, who saw the struggle
In the boat that took off from the ship, manned by the strongest,
Taking me to the island. They seized me and forced me ashore,
And wept. They heard, as the boat drew clear again from the
     rocks,
My final scream of rage, which some have carried
Until the earth has locked their ears against it.
And that for them was the end.
But I, who was left alone in the island's silence,
I lay on the rock in the creek where the sailors placed me,
And slept or drowsed. How should I know how long?

The pain had died and time had lost its meaning.
How should I know how long?
As after death, I lay in peace and triumph,
My only motion, to stretch my left arm outward:
It was satisfactory. The bow was there,
And Troy would not be taken.

Night fell and passed, and day broke clear and cool,
As day breaks now.

This was my home, the winter's gales, the summer,
The cave and the rotting wound,
Where the singing wheel of the seasons became the cycle
Of an endless repeated ritual of sickness and pain.
First the suspicion during the common tasks
Of hewing and killing, or fetching and carrying water;
The hesitation before a memory,
The stumbling thought by which we recognize
That pain is already here, but is still beyond our feeling,
And will soon return to us, returning again
Tomorrow or the next day.
And under the noisy disguises we arouse
To drown and confound that onset, quickly as we turn
To press back a wanton branch, or kick a stone from the way,
The noiseless chant has begun in the heart of the wound,
The heavy procession of pain along the nerve,
The torture-music, the circling and approach
Of the fiery dancers, the days of initiation,
The surge through the heat to the babbling, sweating vault
Of muttering, unanswered questions, on,
Through a catechism of ghosts and a toiling litany,
To the ultimate sanctum of delirium, unremembered,
The recapitulation of the bitterly forgotten,
And then forgotten again in the break of day.

Exhausted and wan in the light of those other daybreaks,
I saw myself, watched my sad days, and prayed
That I might be a grotto below the cliff and the sea,
With the hoarse waters in and around me, forever pelting,
Stilly, forever in place; or a rock, or in winter storms,
A wave which the sea throws perpetually forwards, and
Again and again withdraws, forever in its moving place.
But I am not such a thing. And gliding on a gliding sea,
I must seem to make my choice.

That was my choice which now is my rejection:
The caves of alienation, and the chant

44

Of phantom dancers, the anger and the fury.
And still between rifts of smoke in the acrid darkness,
For a gleaming moment, still the bright daggers besieging
This fiery lump which passes for a heart.
There is one sort of daybreak, a death renewed;
Here is another, a life that glimmers and wakes.
A desert or an ocean perhaps divides them,
Or as rock on rock they lie so close on each other
That our hands can neither persuade them nor tear them apart.
I can only point to one time and speak of it,
And point to another which is different.
One is the buildings of hell, when over a crime
We plaster darkness on darkness, and pray for silence,
While the light grows louder above the disordered days,
The bells with their loud ringing pull down the tower,
And the walled-up entry of death lies exposed and broken.
The other is the beach, unmoving in this other daybreak,
Where Neoptolemus and his companions lie.
The morning mounts and hovers over them.
Time with his patient hand has taken and led them
There where the sailors placed me on that distant morning.
And they lie sleeping, who will bear me back to Troy.
And somewhere between such scenes a god descends
Or a man cries out: 'I am here!'
Unfathomable the light and the darkness between them.

I have lived too long on Lemnos, lonely and desperate,
Quarrelling with conjured demons, with the ghosts
Of the men and women with whom I learned to people
The loneliness and despair; and with those others:
The silent circle
Of the men and women I have been and tried to be.
I cannot look at them now in brake or coomb or fountain,
Silent and watchful round the double mouth of the cave,
As in or out I go; nor if they spoke,
Could bear their agonized frustrated voice
(For they would have one voice only), as in or out I go.
I cannot look at them now, when from over the sea, new ghosts
Lean from the future smiling.

45

Decision is uncertain, made uncertainly
Under ambiguous omens, which here and now cannot question.
Oh, days to come! Give me power to unpick the plots
Which gods and men arrange, to disengage
The gold and silver fragments of their story
And power to let them slip together, accepted,
Their artifice made art.
(I will pick them apart in a year or a generation
After this time. Here they are close together.)

Day breaks: the isle is silent, under the sun,
Which ponders it as though to interpret its silence.
I have changed my mind; or my mind is changed in me.
Unalterable of cliff and water,
The vast ravines are violet, revealing sea.
Here they are close together, the singing fragments
Which gods and men arrange, a chorus of birds and gardens.
The god departs, the men remain, day breaks,
And the bow is ready and burnished.
The arrows are newly fledged with the sun's first feathers.
It is the last still stillness of the morning
Before the first gull screams.
I lie on the rock, the wound is quiet, its death
Is dead within me, and treachery is powerless here.
Under the caves, in the hollows of sheltered beaches
Slowly the sailors wake.
The bushes twitch in the wind on the glowing cliff-sides;
The ghosts dislimn and vanish; the god departs;
My life begins; and a man plants a tree at daybreak.

[1944]

PART II

Lessons of the War
(1946, 1970)

To Alan Michell

Vixi duellis nuper idoneus
Et militavi non sine gloria

1 NAMING OF PARTS

Today we have naming of parts. Yesterday,
We had daily cleaning. And tomorrow morning,
We shall have what to do after firing. But today,
Today we have naming of parts. Japonica
Glistens like coral in all of the neighbouring gardens,
      And today we have naming of parts.

This is the lower sling swivel. And this
Is the upper sling swivel, whose use you will see,
When you are given your slings. And this is the piling swivel,
Which in your case you have not got. The branches
Hold in the gardens their silent, eloquent gestures,
      Which in our case we have not got.

This is the safety-catch, which is always released
With an easy flick of the thumb. And please do not let me
See anyone using his finger. You can do it quite easy
If you have any strength in your thumb. The blossoms
Are fragile and motionless, never letting anyone see
      Any of them using their finger.

And this you can see is the bolt. The purpose of this
Is to open the breech, as you see. We can slide it
Rapidly backwards and forwards: we call this
Easing the spring. And rapidly backwards and forwards
The early bees are assaulting and fumbling the flowers:
      They call it easing the Spring.

They call it easing the Spring: it is perfectly easy
If you have any strength in your thumb: like the bolt,
And the breech, and the cocking-piece, and the point of balance,
Which in our case we have not got; and the almond-blossom
Silent in all of the gardens and the bees going backwards and
   forwards,
      For today we have naming of parts.

[1942]

49

2 JUDGING DISTANCES

Not only how far away, but the way that you say it
Is very important. Perhaps you may never get
The knack of judging a distance, but at least you know
How to report on a landscape: the central sector,
The right of arc and that, which we had last Tuesday,
         And at least you know

That maps are of time, not place, so far as the army
Happens to be concerned—the reason being,
Is one which need not delay us. Again, you know
There are three kinds of tree, three only, the fir and the poplar,
And those which have bushy tops to; and lastly
         That things only seem to be things.

A barn is not called a barn, to put it more plainly,
Or a field in the distance, where sheep may be safely grazing.
You must never be over-sure. You must say, when reporting:
At five o'clock in the central sector is a dozen
Of what appear to be animals; whatever you do,
         Don't call the bleeders *sheep*.

I am sure that's quite clear; and suppose, for the sake of
   example,
The one at the end, asleep, endeavours to tell us
What he sees over there to the west, and how far away,
After first having come to attention. There to the west,
On the fields of summer the sun and the shadows bestow
         Vestments of purple and gold.

The still white dwellings are like a mirage in the heat,
And under the swaying elms a man and a woman
Lie gently together. Which is, perhaps, only to say
That there is a row of houses to the left of arc,
And that under some poplars a pair of what appear to be
   humans
         Appear to be loving.

Well that, for an answer, is what we might rightly call
Moderately satisfactory only, the reason being,
Is that two things have been omitted, and those are important.
The human beings, now: in what direction are they,
And how far away, would you say? And do not forget
        There may be dead ground in between.

There may be dead ground in between; and I may not have got
The knack of judging a distance; I will only venture
A guess that perhaps between me and the apparent lovers
(Who, incidentally, appear by now to have finished)
At seven o'clock from the houses, is roughly a distance
        Of about one year and a half.

[1943]

Those of you that have got through the rest, I am going to
      rapidly
Devote a little time to showing you, those that can master it,
A few ideas about tactics, which must not be confused
With what we call strategy. Tactics is merely
The mechanical movement of bodies, and that is what we mean
      by it.
            Or perhaps I should say: by them.

Strategy, to be quite frank, you will have no hand in.
It is done by those up above, and it merely refers to
The larger movements over which we have no control.
But tactics are also important, together or single.
You must never forget that suddenly, in an engagement,
            You may find yourself alone.

This brown clay model is a characteristic terrain
Of a simple and typical kind. Its general character
Should be taken in at a glance, and its general character
You can see at a glance it is somewhat hilly by nature,
With a fair amount of typical vegetation
            Disposed at certain parts.

Here at the top of the tray, which we might call the northwards,
Is a wooded headland with a crown of bushy-topped trees on;
And proceeding downwards or south we take in at a glance
A variety of gorges and knolls and plateaus and basins and
      saddles,
Somewhat symmetrically put, for easy identification.
            And here is our point of attack.

But remember of course it will not be a tray you will fight on,
Nor always by daylight. After a hot day, think of the night
Cooling the desert down, and you still moving over it:
Past a ruined tank or a gun, perhaps, or a recently dead friend,
Lying about somewhere: it might quite well be that.
            It isn't always a tray.

And even this tray is different to what I had thought.
These models are somehow never always the same; the reason
I do not know how to explain quite. Just as I do not know
Why there is always someone at this particular lesson
Who always starts crying. Now will you kindly
        Empty those blinking eyes?

I thank you. I have no wish to seem impatient.
I know it is all very hard, but you would not like,
To take a simple example, to take for example,
This place we have thought of here, you would not like
To find yourself face to face with it, and you not knowing
        What there might be inside?

Very well then: suppose this is what you must capture.
It will not be easy, not being very exposed,
Secluded away like it is, and somewhat protected
By a typical formation of what appear to be bushes,
So that you cannot see, as to what is concealed inside,
        As to whether it is friend or foe.

And so, a strong feint will be necessary in this connection.
It will not be a tray, remember. It may be a desert stretch
With nothing in sight, to speak of. I have no wish to be
    inconsiderate,
But I see there are two of you now, commencing to snivel.
I cannot think where such emotional privates can come from.
        Try to behave like men.

I thank you. I was saying: a thoughtful deception
Is always somewhat essential in such a case. You can see
That if only the attacker can capture such an emplacement
The rest of the terrain is his: a key-position, and calling
For the most resourceful manoeuvres. But that is what tactics is.
        Or I should say rather: are.

Let us begin then and appreciate the situation.
I am thinking especially of the point we have been considering,
Though in a sense everything in the whole of the terrain
Must be appreciated. I do not know what I have said
To upset so many of you. I know it is a difficult lesson.
        Yesterday we had a man faint.

53

But I have never known as many as *five* in a single intake,
Unable to cope with this lesson. I think you had better
Fall out, all five, and sit at the back of the room,
Being careful not to talk. The rest will close up.
Perhaps it was me saying 'a dead friend', earlier on?
      Well, some of us live.

And I never know why, whenever we get to tactics,
Men either laugh or cry, though neither being strictly called for.
But perhaps I have started too early with a difficult problem?
We will start again, further north, with a simpler assault.
Are you ready? Is everyone paying attention?
      Very well, then. Here are two hills.

[1950]

4 UNARMED COMBAT

In due course of course you will all be issued with
Your proper issue; but until tomorrow,
You can hardly be said to need it; and until that time,
We shall have unarmed combat. I shall teach you
The various holds and rolls and throws and breakfalls
        Which you may sometimes meet.

And the various holds and rolls and throws and breakfalls
Do not depend on any sort of weapon,
But only on what I might coin a phrase and call
The ever-important question of human balance,
And the ever-important need to be in a strong
        Position at the start.

There are many kinds of weakness about the body,
Where you would least expect, like the ball of the foot.
But the various holds and rolls and throws and breakfalls
Will always come in useful. And never be frightened
To tackle from behind: it may not be clean to do so,
        But this is global war.

So give them all you have, and always give them
As good as you get; it will always get you somewhere
(You may not know it, but you can tie a Jerry
Up without a rope; it is one of the things I shall teach you).
Nothing will matter if only you are ready for him.
        The readiness is all.

The readiness is all. How can I help but feel
I have been here before? But somehow then,
I was the tied-up one. How to get out
Was always then my problem. And even if I had
A piece of rope I was always the sort of person
        Who threw the rope aside.

And in my time I have given them all I had,
Which was never as good as I got, and it got me nowhere.

And the various holds and rolls and throws and breakfalls
Somehow or other I always seemed to put
In the wrong place. And as for war, my wars
    Were global from the start.

Perhaps I was never in a strong position,
Or the ball of my foot got hurt, or I had some weakness
Where I had least expected. But I think I see the point:
While awaiting a proper issue, we must learn the lesson
Of the ever-important question of human balance.
    It is courage that counts.

Things may be the same again; and we must fight
Not in the hope of winning but rather of keeping
Something alive: so that when we meet our end,
It may be said that we tackled wherever we could,
That battle-fit we lived, and though defeated,
    Not without glory fought.

[1945]

5   RETURNING OF ISSUE

Tomorrow will be your last day here. Someone is speaking:
A familiar voice, speaking again at all of us.
And beyond the windows (it is inside now, and autumn)
On a wind growing daily harsher, small things to the earth
Are turning and whirling, small. Tomorrow will be
      Your last day here,

But not we hope for always. You cannot see through the
  windows
If they are leaves or flowers. We hope that many of you
Will be coming back for good. (Silence, and stupefaction.)
The coarsening wind and the things whirling upon it
Scour that rough stamping-ground where we so long
      Have spent our substance,

As the trees are spending theirs. How much of mine have I spent,
Father, oh father? How sorry we are to lose you
I do not have to say, since the sergeant-major
Has said it, the RSM has said it, and the colonel
Has sent over a message to say that he also says it.
      Everyone sorry to lose us,

And you, oh father, father, once sorry too. I think
I can honestly say you are one and all of you now:
Soldiers. (Silence, and disbelief.) A fact that will stand you
In pretty good stead in the various jobs you go back to.
I wish you the best of luck. (Silence.) And all of you know
      You can think of us here, as *home*.

As home: a home we shall any of you welcome you back to.
Most of you have, I know, some sort of work waiting for you,
And the rest of you now being, thanks to us, fit and able,
Will be bound to find something. I begin to be in want.
Would any citizen of this country send me
      Into his fields? And

Before I finalize: one thing about tomorrow
I must make perfectly clear. Tomorrow is clear already:

I saw myself once, but now am by God forbidden
To see myself so, as the one who went evil ways,
Till he determined, in time of famine, to seek
      His father's home.

Autumn is later down there: it should now be the time
Of vivacious triumph in the fruitful fields.
As he approached, he ran over his speeches of sorrow,
Not less of truth for being long rehearsed,
The last distilment from a long and inward
      Discourse of heartbreak. And

The first thing you do, after first thing tomorrow morning,
Is, those that have not been previously detailed to do so,
Which I think is the case in most cases, is a systematic
Returning of issue. It is all-important
You should restore to store one of every store issued.
      And in the event of two, two.

And I, as ever late, shall never know that lifted fear
When the small hard-working master of those fields
Looked up. I trembled. But his heart came out to me
With a shout of compassion. And all my speech was only:
'Father, I have sinned against heaven, and am no more worthy
      To be called thy son'.

But if I cried it, father, you could not hear me now,
Where now you lie, crumpled in that small grave
Like any withering dog. Your fields are sold and built on,
Your lanes are filled with husks the swine reject.
I scoop them in my hands. I have earned no more; and more
      I shall not inherit. And

A careful check will be made of every such object
That was issued to each personnel originally,
And checked at issue. And let me be quite implicit:
That no accoutrements, impedimentas, fittings, or military
  garments
May be taken as souvenirs. The one exception is shirts,
      And whatever you wear underneath.

These may be kept, those that wish. But the rest of the issue
Must be returned, except who intend to rejoin
In regular service. (Silence.) Which involves a simple procedure
I will explain in a simple group to those that rejoin.
Now, how many will that be? (Silence.) No one? No one at all?
      I see. I have up to now

Spoken with the utmost of mildness. I speak so still,
But it does seem to me a bit of a bloody pity,
A bit un-bloody-feeling, after the all
We have bloody done for you, you should sit on your dumb
   bloody arses,
Just waiting like bloody milksops till I bloody dismiss you.
      (Silence, embarrassed, but silent.)

And am I to break it, father, to break this silence?
Is there no bloody *man* among you? Not one bloody single *one*?
I will break the silence, father. Yes, sergeant, *I* will stay
In a group of one. Father, be proud of me.
Oh splendid, man! And for Christ's sake, tell them all,
      Why you are doing this.

Why am I doing this? And is it too late to say no?
Come speak out, man: tell us, and shame these bastards.
I hope to shame no one, sergeant, in simply wishing
To remain a personnel. I have been such a thing before.
It was good, and simple; and it was the best I could do.
      Here is a man, men! (Silence.

Silence, indeed.) How could I tell them, now,
I have nowhere else to go? How could I say
I have no longer gift or want; or how describe
The inexplicable tears that filled my eyes
When the poor sergeant said: 'After the all
      We have bloody done for you'?

Goodbye for ever, father, after the all you have done for me.
Soon I must start to forget you; but not to forget
That reconcilement, never enacted between us,
Which should have been ours, under the autumn sun.

I can see it and feel it now, clearer than daylight, clearer
    For one brief moment, now,

Than even the astonished faces of my fellows,
The sergeant's uneasy smile, the trees, the relief at choosing
To learn once more the things I shall one day teach:
A rhetoric instead of words; instead of a love, the use
Of accoutrements, impedimenta, and fittings, and military
    garments,
        And harlots, and riotous living.

                                                    [1970]

PART III

Uncollected poems
(1950–1975)

THE CHANGELING

The child, one evening, looks
Into the sudden bloom
Of sunset chimney and roof,
And his reddened printed page
Seems to afford him proof
That he is of another age,
A changeling whisked from the grace
And the ceremonious kiss
Of a noble time and place.
He turns to the darkening room,
The garret grate, the books,
And backed by the bright sky,
He whispers into the gloom:
'What is here in my book is true.
I was changed at my birth. I am I,
And was never born for you.'

Later, in love, beneath
A lamp in a fading street,
Late lit in the summer dusk,
He watches, and waits, and fails.
Expected, hurrying feet
Approach, are strange, pass,
Die away on the paving-stones,
And silence again prevails.
He waits, and cannot believe
In the street's emptiness:
'Since I was given breath,
I was surely born to live.
Why am I tied to a death?'

On a still later day,
A soldier at his post,
He stands in a freezing dawn.
The garret, the lamp, come back,
Pass, salute, return
To a mind on sentry-go.

The scalding tears fall
And frost on the cold bone.
In the ending night alone,
He mouths a silent call
Into the still-born day:
'My life, my life, my life,
Beyond the barrack-wall,
Where are you drifting away?'

Through love and soldierhood
He passes along his track,
Unfinding the sought good;
So that his soul would,
If you could see it, be bent
To a strange anguished shape.
Until in the fall of peace
His days at last relent,
The soldier's tasks cease,
Love takes him by his hand,
And the child to exile bred
Comes to his native land.

And comes, at last, to stand
On his scented evening lawn
Under his flowering limes,
Where dim in the dusk and high,
His mansion is proudly set,
And the single light burns
In the room where his sweet young wife
Waits in his ancient bed.
The stable clock chimes.
And he to his house draws near,
And on the threshold turns,
With a silent glance to convey
Up to his summer sky,
Where his first pale stars appear:
'All this is false. And I
Am an interloper here.'

[1950]

AUBADE

Then the first bird at dawn, *It is her day!* he cried
At once another, *This is her day!* replied.
And all the sentinels of the morning waiting there
Sang and rose singing up through the shining air.

And the first tree, *What is this sound*, he said,
That breaks and shakes the air above my head?
It is her day! came the bright leaves' reply,
In millions glittering under the singing sky.

      Shine, silent flower,
             Brilliant bird, sing out . . .
      Shine, field and lawn,
             Glittering song, fly on . . .
      Parkland and fell;
      Shine, silent stream,
      River, rock, shore;
             Dazzling tides, run bright . . .
      Mountain and hill,
             Echoing sky, resound . . .
      Shine through this day.

May the whole morning of England sing her praise.
Crown her with light, crown with delight her days.
Let her long day, let her long day extend,
Nor dark, nor dark, upon her earth descend:
When bird and leaf and flower in night are stilled,
Let her triumphant sky with the light of her stars be filled.

[1953]

THE AUCTION SALE

Within the great grey flapping tent
The damp crowd stood or stamped about;
And some came in, and some went out
To drink the moist November air;
None fainted, though a few looked spent
And eyed some empty unbought chair.
It was getting on. And all had meant
Not to go home with empty hands
But full of gain, at little cost,
Of mirror, vase, or vinaigrette.
Yet often, after certain sales,
Some looked relieved that they had lost,
Others, at having won, upset.
Two men from London sat apart,
Both from the rest and each from each,
One man in grey and one in brown.
And each ignored the other's face,
And both ignored the endless stream
Of bed and bedside cabinet.
They gazed intent upon the floor,
And both were strangers in that place.

Two other men, competing now,
Locals, whom everybody knew,
In shillings genially strove
For some small thing in ormolu.
Neither was eager; one looked down
Blankly at eighty-four, and then
Rallied again at eighty-eight,
And took it off at four pound ten.
The loser grimly shook his fist,
But friendly, there was nothing meant.
Little gained was little missed,
And there was smiling in the tent.

The auctioneer paused to drink,
And wiped his lips and looked about,
And held in whispered colloquy

The clerk, who frowned and seemed to think,
And murmured: 'Why not do it next?'
The auctioneer, though full of doubt,
Unacquiescent, rather vexed,
At last agreed, and at his sign
Two ministrants came softly forth
And lifted in an ashen shroud
Something extremely carefully packed,
Which might have been some sort of frame,
And was a picture-frame in fact.
They steadied it gently and with care,
And held it covered, standing there.

The auctioneer again looked round
And smiled uneasily at friends,
And said: 'Well, friends, I have to say
Something I have not said today:
There's a reserve upon this number.
It is a picture which though unsigned
Is thought to be of the superior kind,
So I am sure you gentlemen will not mind
If I tell you at once, before we start,
That what I have been asked to say
Is, as I have said, to say:
There's a reserve upon this number.'
There was a rustle in that place,
And some awoke as though from slumber.
Anxious disturbance fluttered there;
And as if summoned to begin,
Those who had stepped outside for air
Retrieved themselves, and stepped back in.

The ministrants, two local boys,
Experienced in this sort of work,
And careful not to make too much noise,
Reached forward to unhook the shroud
That slowly opening fell away
And on the public gaze released
The prospect of a great gold frame
Which through the reluctant leaden air

Flashed a mature unsullied grace
Into the faces of the crowd.
And there was silence in that place.

> *Effulgent in the Paduan air,*
> *Ardent to yield the Venus lay*
> *Naked upon the sunwarmed earth.*
> *Bronze and bright and crisp her hair,*
> *By the right hand of Mars caressed,*
> *Who sunk beside her on his knee,*
> *His mouth toward her mouth inclined,*
> *His left hand near her silken breast.*
> *Flowers about them sprang and twined,*
> *Accomplished Cupids leaped and sported,*
> *And three, with dimpled arms enlaced*
> *And brimming gaze of stifled mirth,*
> *Looked wisely on at Mars's nape,*
> *While others played with horns and pikes,*
> *Or smaller objects of like shape.*

And there was silence in that place.
They gazed in silence; silently
The wind dropped down, no longer shook
The flapping sides and gaping holes.
And some moved back, and others went
Closer, to get a better look.

> *In ritual, amorous delay,*
> *Venus deposed her sheltering hand*
> *Where her bright belly's aureate day*
> *Melted to dusk about her groin;*
> *And, as from words that Mars had said*
> *Into that hidden, subtle ear,*
> *She turned away her shining head.*

The auctioneer cleared his throat,
And said: 'I am sure I'm right in feeling
You will not feel it at all unfair
For what when all is said and done
Is a work of very artistic painting
And not to be classed with common lumber,

And anyway extremely rare,
You will not feel it at all unfair
If I mention again before proceeding,
There's a reserve upon this number.'
Someone was clearly heard to say:
'What, did I hear him say *reserve?'*
(Meaning, of course, a different meaning.)
This was a man from Sturminster,
Renowned for a quiet sense of fun,
And there was laughter in that place,
Though not, of course, from everyone.

> *A calm and gentle mile away,*
> *Among the trees a river ran*
> *Boated with blue and scarlet sails;*
> *A towered auburn city stood*
> *Beyond them on the burnished heights,*
> *And afar off and over all*
> *The azure day for mile on mile*
> *Uncoiled towards the Dolomites.*

The auctioneer said:
'I very much fear I have to say
I'm afraid we cannot look all day.
The reserve is seven hundred pounds.
Will anyone offer me seven fifty?
Seven thirty? Twenty-five?
Thank you, sir. Seven twenty-five.'
It was the man in brown who nodded,
Soon to be joined by him in grey.
The bidding started quietly.
No one from locally joined in.
Left to the men from London way,
The auctioneer took proper pride,
And knew the proper way to guide
By pause, by silence, and by tapping,
The bidding towards a proper price.
And each of the two with unmoved face
Would nod and pause and nod and wait.
And there was tension in that place.

And still within the Paduan field,
The silent summer scene stood by,
The sails, the hill-tops, and the sky,
And the bright warmth of Venus' glance
That had for centuries caught the eye
Of whosoever looked her way,
And now caught theirs, on this far day.

Two people only did not look.
They were the men so calmly nodding,
Intently staring at the floor;
Though one of them, the one in brown,
Would sometimes slowly lift his gaze
And stare up towards the canvas roof,
Whereat a few men standing near
Inquiring eyes would also raise
To try to see what he was seeing.
The bidding mounted steadily
With silent nod or murmured yes
And passed the fifteen hundred mark,
And well beyond, and far beyond,
A nodding strife without success,
Till suddenly, with one soft word,
Something unusual occurred.

The auctioneer had asked politely,
With querying look and quiet smile:
'Come then, may I say two thousand?'
There was the customary pause,
When suddenly, with one soft word,
Another voice was strangely heard
To join in, saying plainly: 'Yes.'
Not their voices, but a third.
Everyone turned in some surprise
To look, and see, and recognize
A young man who some time ago
Had taken a farm out Stalbridge way,
A very pleasant young man, but quiet,
Though always a friendly word to say,
Though no one in the dealing line,

But quiet and rather unsuccessful,
And often seen about the place
At outings or on market-day,
And very polite and inoffensive,
And *quiet*, as anyone would tell you,
But not from round here in any case.

The auctioneer, in some surprise,
Said: 'Please, sir, did I hear you say
Yes to two thousand? Is that bid?
Twenty hundred am I bid?'
The two were silent, and the third,
The young man, answered plainly: 'Yes.
Yes. Two thousand. Yes, I did.'
Meaning that he had said that word.
'Ah, yes. Yes, thank you, sir,' concurred
The auctioneer, surprised, but glad
To know that he had rightly heard,
And added: 'Well, then, I may proceed.
I am bid two thousand for this picture.
Any advance upon that sum?
Any advance upon two thousand?
May I say two thousand twenty?
Twenty? Thirty? Thank you, sir.
May I say forty? Thank you, sir.
Fifty? You, sir? Thank you, sir.'

And now instead of two, the three
Competed in the bargaining.
There was amazement in that place,
But still it gave, as someone said,
A sort of interest to the thing.
The young man nodded with the others,
And it was seen his nice young face,
Had lost its flush and now was white,
And those who stood quite near to him
Said (later, of course, they did not speak
While the bidding was going on)
That on his brow were beads of sweat,
Which as he nodded in acceptance
Would, one or two, fall down his cheek.

And in the tightening atmosphere
Naked upon the sunwarmed earth
Pauses were made and eyebrows raised,
Answered at last by further nods,
Ardent to yield the nods resumed
Venus upon the sunwarmed nods
Abandoned Cupids danced and nodded
His mouth towards her bid four thousand
Four thousand, any advance upon,
And still beyond four thousand fifty
Unrolled towards the nodding *sun.*

But it was seen, and very quickly,
That after four thousand twenty-five,
The man from over Stalbridge way
Did not respond, and from that point
He kept his silent gaze averted,
To show he would not speak again.
And it was seen his sweating face,
Which had been white, was glowing red,
And had a look almost of pain.

> *Oh hand of Venus, hand of Mars.*
> *Oh ardent mouth, oh burnished height,*
> *Oh blue and scarlet gentle sails,*
> *Oh Cupids smiling in the dance,*
> *Oh unforgotten, living glance,*
> *Oh river, hill and flowering plain,*
> *Oh ever-living dying light*

He had a look almost of pain.
The rest was quickly done. The bids
Advanced at slowly slackening pace
Up to four thousand eighty-five.
And at this point the man in grey
Declined his gaze upon the floor
And kept it there, as though to say
That he would bid no more that day.
It was quite clear he had not won,
This man in grey, though anyone
Practised to read the human face
Might on his losing mouth descry

What could no doubt be termed a smile.
While on the face of him in brown
A like expertness might discern
Something that could be termed a frown.

There was a little faint applause.

The auctioneer sighed with joy,
The customary formalities
Were quickly over, and the strangers
Nodding a brief goodbye departed.
Venus and Mars were carefully veiled.
The auctioneer went on and proffered
Vase and table, chair and tray.
Bids of a modest kind were offered,
The traffic of a normal day.
A little later it was seen
The young man too had slipped away.
Which was, of course, to be expected.
Possibly there was nothing else
There at the sale to take his fancy.
Or possibly he even might
Be feeling ashamed at intervening,
Though possibly not, for after all,
He had certainly been within his right.

At all events, an hour later,
Along the Stalbridge road a child
Saw the young man and told her mother,
Though not in fact till some days after,
That she had seen him in the dusk,
Not walking on the road at all,
But striding beneath the sodden trees;
And as she neared she saw that he
Had no covering on his head,
And did not seem to see her pass,
But went on, through the soaking grass,
Crying. That was what she said.

Bitterly, she later added.

Crying bitterly, she said.

[1956]

73

Knowing that the only way left to him now was to wander, and
    wander forever,
        Oedipus cried for his exile; it had been promised him.
They had sworn to banish him forever from where he had once
    been
        King. But the order was somehow ungiven, and to
        banish himself would be flight.
'Deprive me of choice,' he said, 'I would choose wrongly again.'
        His only choice was to sleep on a bed of stone,
Unpillowed, and never indoors; and this was not penance, but
    fear.
        And indeed he had reason for fear; once, torn from a
        dream,
He heard his own voice come towards him, cleaving
        The remnants of sleep, saying: *Love is love,*
Whoever has felt it, for whom: and, after a pause,
        Adding, now fully awake: *Oh men, do you think*
I do not love her still? And he heard his heart weeping
        Thick black tears into his bowels, burning.

'I had pulled out,' he said, 'with my eyes, one power to weep,
        And I grew used to those unweeping sockets,
And learned to weep elsewhere a grotesque new weeping
        That cut like salted swords. But I did not always weep.
There were stillness and silence also. And once, in a deeper
    silence,
        Once only, a deeper dream. (Of pillared Delphi,
The dark ravine at the crossroads, the dusky sunlight,
        The galloping gates of Thebes; and at my back, once
        only,
A faceless, unangered figure looked up from his dying, and said:
        'It was I who was in the way, but why must you kill
        me?
Why must you kill a sorry, travelling stranger, oh child?
        We could even have loved one another; but now you
        have killed me.'
And he continued, continued his dying, and I continued
        To the welcoming gates of Thebes.) This second dream

Was deep, beyond reach of tears, lonely in itself, and helpless.
        But in the end did not this also comfort,

'And make the stone bed restful? I grew used to the days,
        Grew used to the distant thunder of my two sons,
Trying their horses, grew used to their deepening voices.
        I could bear at last without trembling the voice of my
            younger daughter,
And the voice of that other, my beautiful, burning-hearted,
        My darling, my sweet-souled girl.
Things at their worst had ceased; the sun and the air around me
        Could just be borne, and my wish for exile vanished.

'Was it for this they had waited? Apparently.
        For it was on one of those days when, the Theban
            summer, declining,
Admits November, and the solstice is not very near,
        That I felt a cloud go over the sun, and the guards at
            my shoulder,
Murmuring kindly that God had spoken, and that He had said:
        It is time. The roads are empty, the ways of the desert
Should be cruel enough by now. On the cooling winds from
    Athens,
        The eagles are wintrily swinging, and the caves will
            offer no solace.
It is time, oh men. I am ready. You may open the gates for him
    now.'

[1969]

THE RIVER

Our tasks of the night go on, our ritual, our dance.
Our flames go up, reflected in the black, slow river.
Here you must think we are happy and fulfilled—
        You who still wander

On that other side of the river, for whom, in the fated intrigue
Of the years and the days and the hours, it is not yet time
To set your foot on the silent, crowded raft
        Of the all-expectant.

Perfervid lips here babble, and hands caress.
Your words will mingle with them, your hands reach out.
You will not be alone, you will only be one of the many
        Who are not alone here,

In this sorrowful place, where I with a failing blood
Seek out in this dark place for one yet darker.
And pace the muddy shore, the slow ripple glaring,
        And scan the distance

To where *you* stand, your features already reflecting
What they cannot yet absorb, our hectic lights,
And discerning never the scores of ardent eyes
        That are turned toward you;

And discerning never the one who, bent in a separate silence,
Prays in the dark to become the one who is chosen
And sent from the flames of this raucous side of Acheron
        To conduct you over.

[1970]

76

THREE WORDS

What strangeness lies unseen behind our words
    And creeps out in protest if we ever chance to disturb them!
When did I find that the words I had always used
    In every poem were 'suddenly' and 'forever'?

Perhaps in one of those many vacancies
    Of the shuttered mind, the eyes and mouth unsmiling,
And nothing to say, the damnation of nothing to say:
    Perhaps it was then, as with pleading perhaps, the small
        word 'silent'
Followed them, took my hand gently, saying 'Do not forget me:
    I have been also yours.'

                 And suddenly I knew
That these three words would perhaps pursue me forever,
    Inescapable, watchful, loitering at a steady distance.

And with that there came a nonchalant acceptance
    That I would never easily use these words again,
Which did not matter, nor did even the sense
    Of bitter weariness and humiliation.

I saw the Freudian catch: it was even a little comic:
    We are suddenly born: and every poem is birth.
We face our life forever: and every poem
    That is ever spelt must face the future forever,
And perhaps forever in silence. So much, alas, for words.

    (And I have once suddenly known I had lost you forever.
 And have elsewhere suddenly known I would love you forever.
    And there will be two occasions, and those not together,
When you and I will be suddenly silent forever.)

                                  [1970]

THE TOWN ITSELF

And this is Verona, the city of a long-held dream.
Occasions drew me to you, but too late.
I wander about you, unregarded, lost.
The courteous banners of welcome have been folded away.
I see you, now, close to: I know you at last, you me.

I am apprehensive of what I most expect:
That my sojourn-permit, before it has expired,
May yet be taken from me, on some unprepared-for day.

And I had not known that the weather, in what seemed,
At first, unchangeably sought out by the sun,
Could be so variable. And when you are sad, my darling,
No words of mine can alter your clouded skies.
I do not inhabit you. I am no source of joy.
I shall never have the freedom of your city,
Or be an addition to your amenities.

Sometimes the traffic stops; there are strikes; the threat of famine
And homelessness stands in your public squares.
I have come to a place where I have nothing to give,
And you cannot feed yet one more useless mouth.
You have your own, and native ones, to feed.

There are moments when almost martial law is declared,
A curfew set on my love and my concern.
I know such things have been imposed before
And suddenly lifted, with the streets again *en fête*
Under your sun. But by now I know
I shall never be accepted as a citizen:
I am still, and shall always be, a stranger here.
I could endure this, and ask nothing more.
But there is something in your own despairs, my love,
That makes me also know
I am in some way, an intolerable suspect,
And on some day, not long to be postponed,
The police will knock at the door, and I shall be told to go.

[1974]

78

THE BLISSFUL LAND

Le temple est en ruine au haut du promontoire . . .
Hérédia

I

I knew I must go again to that blissful land,
But I made my choice: I would go to it in such a season
As I had never known there, autumn or winter.

I have a capable heart, but I would not let it bear
To see that place again in the honey of summer or spring.
With a murderous delight, I knew that in mid-sorrow
I wanted to see that land impoverish itself in the onset of autumn,
Or in the grimy fists of winter be clenched, and, if possible, torn.

2

I had forgotten that in that blissful land
Winter but rarely came.

There was no snow, no storm.

There was only my own shame
And consternation that the clouds should break apart,
And sunlight flood the bays and promontories
And the sea compose itself to smiles of welcome.

3

Well: since this unlooked-for winter-summer vacancy
Must be sometime or other cleanly learned and loved,
I would love it, cleanly, now. Perhaps I could learn it later:
Perhaps it could live in me, and I in it:
Solitary, emptied, charmless and dispossessed—
(I wondered at that word, so easily come by:
I was 'dispossessed': and yet it did not deprive me.
                              I could not but love that light,
That irresistible, seductive glow
Which led or followed me wherever I went,
And—as I knew it must—finally drew me
To climb our well-known hill.)

79

4

They were there still:
On the promontory, the gun and the broken fort;
Our bench of stone, the grass-beknotted floor,
The bushes, and a yellow winter-flower we cannot have seen
  before.
And I looked from high on the warm familiar sea
And heard behind me that beloved rustling smile
Of tree and bush and flower and flower and bush and tree;
I turned and also smiled, as if we were hand in hand.

It was not as I had thought.

                    For the other forces of that blissful land
That I had never known, revealed themselves,

They were not as I had thought.

5

Breathless they seemed, and a frost grinned on the stone.
Converging they seemed, slowly upon that spot.
They stared at our stone bench.
                    (Oh, for the love of God remember,
I had come in this last hour to believe that everything
Inside this land still loved and would love me always.)

I have said: I turned. Trees, stone, and broken headland,
Stone, archway, earth, stone, grass, stone and now-roaring sea
Saw me for the first time, and saw my face, saw me.
They paused in concerted silence.
                    I saw them, and they saw me.
They assessed me, as it were,
Then murmured among themselves, seeming to choose a
  spokesman
(It was not a light confabulation that they held)
And at last their chosen spokesman, at a common signal
That it should speak for the whole of that winter concourse
In its rigid courtroom of damnation and grinning stone,

An icy wind slowly approached me, paused, searched my face,
And screamed in rancour, contempt, and disappointment:
'It was not *you* that we wanted! How dared you to come here
     alone?'

[1974]

FOUR PEOPLE

At the thinning end of her time, she wanders, still not idly,
Along the esplanade, skirting the sunned beach below her,
With her, two dogs, unleashed, and sometimes other creatures:
At the thinning end of her time
                    Pierfrancesco,
As is his way, has instituted inquiries. These have disclosed
She is a former aristocrat, who has, it seems, lost all,
And who stumbles in others' clothing, as it were blindly,
But with some purpose still, skirting the summer beach.
Sometimes she halts, and gropes through a ten-page letter,
A plaintive fragment perhaps from a still insistent past
By her unwanted now.
                    Pierfrancesco
Has inquired further, and has further found:
She is now, it seems, only a protectress of animals,
Of the cats and dogs who dawdle along behind her,
Some of whom, when she dies,
Soon after will also die, at the strangeness of their lives without
    her,
But who now all know her, and instantly run towards her
At the sound of her harsh, soft cries.
We watch her, daily,
Pierfrancesco smiles, as he watches me watch her.
I turn and smile to him, and his smile changes.

We also daily watch
The kindly, sick young man who always passes her
Without salutation (they do not know one another)
And who comes, day after day, to the restaurant-tables
With a handful of gleaming postcards, of places across the bay
He has doubtless himself not seen.

                    Pierfrancesco
Has asked, and confirmed as much, and much else also.
The young man speaks. 'This one is pretty,' he says,
'And these are also pretty,
Perhaps even more so . . .'

                              (Long sand, and curving hill,
The fortress, the jaunty harbour, and the pinewood,
And actors, acting, at Portovenere,
And other things also pretty, perhaps even more so.)
You speak, and look up and at him,
You see, as often before, as his young glance meets your own,
He too is of those at the thinning end of their time,
Who are still strangely wanting to please,
And have always wanted to please.
                              But today he knows that you know,
And in a moment his misery comes out through his eyes
And passes into your own, leaving in his a look
Of scared apology. He had hoped that you would not know.
But now he knows that you know.
                              He looks towards Pierfrancesco,
Who looks hard at the sea, and bites hard on his nether lip.

And now we all know that we know. And though you slowly
Buy postcards you do not want, conversing expertly
On the beauties of this and that; and though you uncouthly pay
The doomed young man twice over, to still your trouble and his,
(And it does neither) you cannot alter the fact
That he has not much longer to live, that his time, like hers, is
   thinning.

Is that why they never dare to acknowledge each other,
Having so little in common, and so much?

Ten minutes later we see them passing each other.
                                             Pierfrancesco
In all that time has been forcing himself not to cry.

They pass each other, unseeing. Alike they have
Not enough time, and not enough more of these days,
Under this sun, with its long and comforting blaze.

                              83

We see them pass each other. And Pierfrancesco
Turns upon me at last his eyes: they are full of fear and distress,
As he sees in the eyes of someone who loves him, that love,
Unwillingly, and inhumanly,
Become, by a fraction, less.

[1974]

BOCCA DI MAGRA

This must endure,
This which so dazzles us now, and flaunts itself,
Must soon endure
Silence upon the ecstatic shouting voices;
And the benign air chilled that strokes our bodies
Must endure,
Us absent, another December on the sand-dunes
And lonely wincing sunlight on an ice,
Which may form (it is known to have done so before)
On the harmless stream that now
Placidly greets the sea in blue to blue:
All this must endure
Winter.

                             So, God forgive me, must you.
You are poor, my love.

That colour on your cheeks and on your brow
Will blanch again, and the resistless print
Of the claws of the frost will mark them and mar them.
Your voice and mine will leave our joyful echoes
(Spinning, now spinning up into the lighted air)
To the damp absorption of the palisade,
And the pine and the willow-wood,
And emerge, us gone, as the fretful mouthings of winter,
Hoarse in the caverns, or simply muttering
In the damp and rotting constructions mouldering here.
And if from their grovelling slumber
A murmur swells, it will swell not with our warm voices,
But rise and shriek in a whirlwind of blinded crying,
Screaming along the river's bank to greet its companion,
The great impassive cold that already seems to chide us
From the bluffs of Carrara, gashed by the great into greatness.

                           I, too, shall be poor, my love
In a different way. How foreign it is to think
This time next year, if there is a next, we may meet as might
   academics,
And compare the findings which I shall so much dread.

(Am I so loveless, my love, or only trustless?
No, I am neither, my love.) I shall gravely and bravely surmise
And hope that at this thin mouth of the estuary,
The blue to the blue returning,
I shall feel, as last year and this, your warm, good mouth
    beneath mine,
And see, unchanged,
The shy agreeing sweet suggestion in your eyes
As one of us murmurs: 'There are other places than this.'

[1975]

PART IV

From the radio plays
(1947–1979)

from *Moby Dick*

If you touch at the islands. The islands are far away southwards,
And here is the dreadful sight of snowfall on sliding water,
The slow dead bite of the cold, the jaws of the blind ice closing,
The claws distending and binding their fiend's grip tighter and
  tighter.

And my tomorrow came. And worse than the pain in my
  temples,
Or the pain in my frozen hands as I clung to the glassy rigging,
Was the thought of the light round the harbour, the warmth
  feeling out in the darkness,
The voice of the hidden singer. This was the pain I expected.

Their fiend's grip tighter and tighter. In the strangling exile of
  winter,
The iceberg breaking south and far from its proper confines;
Till a link in the ice-chain melts, and the wind for a lulling
  moment
Suspends its roaring song. The spring has begun to enter.

The pain I expected died, in a maze of other tomorrows.
I expected it to die, and the real winter survived it.
And now with its murmur and mocking the spring has survived
  the winter,
I can feel my flesh on my flesh. And nearer and nearer the
  islands.

Whiteness is lovely. Oh, come and go, white angels,
On the snowy stairways of Heaven. Whiteness is lovely then.
Whiteness is lovely as it lies on the city-roofs.
The winter morning is a transfixed delight,
In the still small garden of home. The snowy pearl
Gleams in your ear, and is lovely. Alabaster
Gleams white on breast and thigh in the marble temple

89

Under shine of planet and star. In the days of Caesar,
White stones were joyful days. There are white moons and roses.

We are hunting a white whale.

But what of that whiteness with no house or tree beneath it?
Under the snow, the ice, and under the ice
The white eternal waters gushing in darkness.
Whiteness is also terror. Over the snow,
Under the great blind eye of the Antarctic,
On his white horse the blizzard rides, a shrouded
Figure in the mist, his white voice winding round you.
Under the tropic wave the white shark glides and waits.
Whiteness is terror. The leper's breast and thigh.

We are hunting a white whale.

————————

[CABACO'S SONG]

The white-walled town is far away,
Upon the hills I lie all day,
The shadows on me dance and play;
    I lie and sing,
    I lie and sing . . .

Oh idle joy of heart and mind,
I wake to summer and I find
The towns of sorrow left behind;
    I lie and sing,
    I lie and sing . . .

The sky is all about me spread,
The bee towards the flower is led;
He weaves a silence round my head;
    I lie and sing,
    I lie and sing.

————————

Can you think what that life is like? Again and again,
The enormous creature at bay in his final flurry of blood,
The torn boats in the water, the vast seas rolling
Indifferently over defeat, of creature or man;
The great beast turning, head to the sun, to die;
Lying so great that the windy and creaking vessel
Must be steered and tied to his side as to a harbour.
He will be picked and peeled by midget men.
The giant tackles will strip his body white. Shapeless and bloody,
His swinging garment of flesh will hang from the maintop
And touch the deck . . . Can you think what that life is like?

The reek of blood through the mist, and blood baked in sunlight,
The slither of blood on the deck, and blood in the tempest . . .
The sombre rites performed, can you think of a carcase
Stripped and beheaded, the sharks and the birds around it?
The white mass floating there: the waves breaking on it:
A menace to ships in the dark.

                          Can you think of the weeks
Drifting through sunlight or storm, no vessel spoken,
Or spoken, quickly gone on a jealous quest?

                          Can you think
Of the mad grey lust of a captain, a different quest
Running its course, nightly throughout his brain?

Can you think what that life is like? Even across the sea
The winds blow tales of death, of other deaths
Than the deaths that surround us. Rumour and mystery
Weave a way like a fog about us. Every strangeness
Carries a warning inflection. The small fish in our wake
Leave us to follow another, and that is a portent;
The trumpet drops from the lips of a friendly stranger,
And that means evil. Evil murmurs surround us.

And still the fountain rises in the distance,
Enticement in the sun. The fogs disperse.
Evil and portent, rumour and mystery forgotten,
Again the fiery hunt sets out on its murderous way.

And some return not from that murderous way,
Or worse, return as strangers.

———————————

Oh, higher than albatross soaring, the white-winged goney,
Higher than the wing of bird, oh wing of angel,
Higher than the sight of man, oh sight of God!
See from this point of sky the last far ramparts of Asia,
Bowered by the gilded, the purpled-and-gilded sea.
No motion of wave or sail. Sumatra stilled,
And silent the forests of Java; the gateway of Sunda
Locked in enchanted air. And Bali and Timor
Faint through the glittering mist on the curved edge of the world.

Descend, descend. Till the wave stirs on the ocean,
The wind on the crest of the forest. Descend again,
Through the screaming and soaring of birds, hover and stay
Where the world of ships and men minutely appears,
You cannot miss the ships that miss each other,
Ships that the round earth parts you cannot miss them.
Descend again to our lonely surface world,
The world of shadowed life, where the sharp sun throws
Shadows of men on the decks, of sails on the water.

There is another world, becalmed and charmed
Under the water. Here the leviathan
Innumerably and ponderously keeps
His breeding-ground; here his vast roving courts
Pause in a giant circle,
                     to whose borders,
We with our darts bring fright and consternation.
Yet in the still blue waters at the centre
The young whales suckle calmly,
                          and their great mothers
Float in the heavenly depth; our boat is only
A drifting shape across their upward glance. Our bloody wars
Stir not a ripple round them . . . Central delight;
Eternal mildness of joy.

———————————

We are hunting a white whale.
He is not such a beast as may be caught
Easily, a day's brief chase, the day's surrender.
Night falls, and the foreign stars that set our heaven
Drop closer down, are lifted and borne by the swell,
And splinter and dazzle the sight, as the summer wave
Falls on the summer wave.
And here in the night they onward move, the three,
Ahab, the whale, the sea, our trinity.

The men breathe fitfully in bunk and hammock;
They live as one in the daytime, now at night
They dream as one, as one they stir in their dream.
We are a ship no longer: we are Ahab.
We are one man now, not thirty.
Fears and forebodings we have felt; not now;
One courage leads us on, a single doom
Presses upon us. The chase at last is ours.

Day breaks: the sea is empty;
(Oh, Starbuck's hope!) he is gone, the sea is void,
Smiling benevolently from dawn to noonday.
                              But at that hour,
The ship is wrung with delight. The whale is there,
The sea, intolerably bright, leaps after him,
And the white water round him blinds the sight.
He will not be chased today: he comes to meet us.

I, Ishmael, have seen this . . . I have also seen
This is, not yet, the day we have waited for.
This is defeat again. The leviathan,
A score of lances in his round white sides,
Lashes and beats the water. Ropes, men, harpoons and boats
Are the white whale's drapings now. I, Ishmael, have seen them.
Under the arched, foam-beaten sunlit sky
I have seen Laocoön's agony, and his children
Yearning and torn by the Hydra.
The desperate knives flash in the sun. He sounds.
Are they safe? Are they safe?

                    They are safe,
In the babble and froth of the sea, its master-mystery
Sinks to his depths below them, watching and waiting.
He has drawn first blood and second . . .

———————————

[ISHMAEL'S EPILOGUE]

No, you are gone, oh King . . . All your unwilling servants
Have gone before you, into the whirlpool, down.
And why should I alone escape? Is it only
To tell your story, foolish King?
                    Why do I float alone,
On this magic driftwood? And is it boat or coffin?
I glide alone on a gliding sea; the unharming sharks
Go by, as though with padlocks on their mouths;
My eyes are full of salt and blood: yet the silenced birds
Stay high above me, aloft, in a trance of mercy.
(Oh, let me live!)
                    A day and a night have gone . . .
There are crowded sails, whitened in a new day's light.
Are they bearing toward *me*?
                    They are the sails of the *Rachel*,
Still looking for her dead. (Let me live, oh God!)
                    Even with every hand
Against me, mine against all, even alone . . .
Even alone, if only to tell a story . . .
Even alone (oh thou, fair Christ in Heaven!) even alone . . .
Even alone, *let me live*!

                                        (197

94

from *Pytheas*

Through sun and shower,
Through brake and bower,
Through day and hour
    I go my way;
The wolf cannot stay me,
The snake delay me,
Nor the great bear waylay me:
    I go my way.

I ruffle the raven
I harry the craven,
In every haven
    You find me at play.
And light as a feather,
Or heavy as leather,
Through turncoat weather
    I go my way.

And swelling and lifting,
And pausing and shifting,
Caressing and drifting,
    I go my way.
You cannot bely me,
You cannot defy me,
You cannot deny me,
    I go my way.

———————

Who is our earth's great man? It is Alexander.
Who holds the East in his hands? It is Alexander.
Babylon, Ecbatana, and Maracanda
Were wise before we learned to think. Now they are all
Greek cities. Persia and Egypt: his.
His prowling armies approach a land of mountains
With gilded cities in their steaming valleys.
They call it India. He will call it Greece.
His gaze is steady, and his hand lies gently
Upon the fluttering pulse of greed and fear.
Under his ministrations, unprotesting,
Civilizations die.

The tangled knots that trouble his soldiers' minds
He weaves as simple skeins in a giant whip
Which cracks from Scythia to the Himalayas;
And at his front, a respectful distance before him,
The Indian whore and Persian catamite
Shout out their morning greeting.
While at his back, a respectful distance after,
They come, that dancing galaxy of evening,
The merchants, speculators, and accountants,
The moneylenders with the gleaming teeth,
Ready to put 'the East on its feet again'.

That is his way, not mine.
I do not want to carry our southern gods
Out into northern waters; I do not want
To bring back loot and pale slaves from those lands;
Or to tie between that sunless world and here
The gaudy ribbons of commerce, every year
Growing a little more grubby with grime and sweat
From the anxious hands of the dealers.
I want to see what is there.

————————————

How an early morning departure always uncovers
The daybreaks we never see. The flowers and stones
Have been there all night, tree, grass and flinted wall.
The houses are still, and wrapt in their white stone sleep,
The hills are mute, colour and light of day
Drained into silence. Only the slow wide sky
Moves its great fan of stars over the town.

Oh starry night, fade slowly! Dawn, come not
To stretch your fingers through the heavy streets;
Oh waking shepherd-boy, it is not time
For your cold flute and bell to climb the hill.
Droop still, oh flower; oh dews, melt not in morning.

I, Pytheas, am leaving you. I who have prayed
For this one day, for chance, for speed, for luck,
Would at this final moment delay the hours . . .
But in the East already, in the deserts,
All Alexander's soldiers walk through gold.
I cannot staunch the day. The day must come,
And the highest tower glow, the flood of morning
Creep down the waking trees.

There are, thank God, those other times in history,
Between the ice and the tropic, the years of the oak and the
    windflower,
Dewfall and winding water, years of peace.
A man may wander away, through the still meadows,
Thickets and woodlands, breaking out at evening,
Mild perspiration on his brow and shoulders,
Into new clearings, coming to unknown faces,
And venturing without that cry, that howl from the other ages:
'Forbear, and eat no more!'

                        There are other ages
Flanking those seldom times: the frozen epochs,
Snowfall for ever on congealed and huddled tents,
A trail of death and blood across ice and snow.

Or times when death comes easy, drops from the jungle trees,
Death distilled from the coiling flower, the orchid,
And the jaws of the patient snake.

We know in childhood,
And never for certain after, those epochs of interim calm,
The smooth, slow years. And now: how far a distance,
How far have I come from my troubled, ageing south,
Where even happiness is a resentment,
Where happiness falls off us like a cloak,
Or is deftly removed from our shoulders, and we
Are left unprotected.

Here, in this northern pause,
Easy arrival and easy departure, turning
With a light goodbye, the falling petal's kiss,
Dew on the forehead, smoothness of face and limb,
Bursting through thickets, confident of welcome,
And quick to learn the ways of other tribes,
Here between spring and autumn I have found that lost age
    again.

———————————

Here then at last I stand, Pytheas, a brown-limbed Greek,
Cloaked in a northern weather.
This is the edge of the world.
There is no going on beyond this place.
The nightmare mountains rise; the fog for a moment lifts,
And under the glacial sun, the narrow sea-bays gleam.
It is a ghostly embrace. Does the sea reach out
Its arms to clutch the land, or does the land
Grasp at the roaring sea, and manage only
To hold in its grip a little quieted water?

And they say that men can live there. How do they move?
Shivering down to the waters. How do they breed? Is love
Not frozen in this arctic never-night,
Which is also never day? For the sun
Is never seen and yet is never absent.

98

Thule: a name for ever. *Thule*: a name for nowhere.

The air is a webbed breath, the sky is a veil of whiteness,
The sea is blinded, the lights in the northern sky
Are a fretful silver flicker through the mist.

That is not a land to possess. Those shores will never be
   crowded,
As our shores are. No songs would sound in those bays.
But this is a place to come to. A place which waits,
Which men have always come to, and always will.
They may not pace a yard from their southern houses,
May live for ever ostensibly bowered by the vine,
The olive and ilex. But at some time or other,
This they can not escape: the reaches of Thule,
The sharp black rock in the ice; the miles and miles,
And miles and miles of slowly darkening mist.
At the end of a hill-road; and at the end of a life;
And at the end of love, and at the end of youth;
And at the end of evening. Here can be there for them.
In taking report of this place, I only take them
A name for that which they have always known.
Others will come after me, with or without aim,
And will leave in the tracks of Time a known or an unknown
   name.
And here at their journey's end they will know what they came
   to seek.
And I have got my answer.
                    I, Pytheas, a brown-limbed Greek.

from *The Monument*

[LITTLE BIRD, MY LITTLE DOVE]

Little bird, my little dove,
Little dove, as white as snow:
See, I have you in my hands,
And I shall not let you go.
And I shall not let you go.
And I shall not let you go.

from *The Great Desire I Had*

Sing lullaby, as women do,
Wherewith to bring their babes to rest.
And lullaby can I sing too,
As womanly as can the best.
With lullaby they still the child,
And if I be not much beguil'd,
Full many wanton babes have I
Which must be still'd with lullaby.

First lullaby my youthful years,
It is now time to go to bed,
For crooked age and hoary hairs
Have won the haven within my head,
With lullaby then youth be still,
With lullaby content thy will,
Since courage quails, and comes behind,
Go sleep, and so beguile thy mind.

from *The Streets of Pompeii*

[FRANCESCA AND ATTILIO]

He sleeps, Attilio sleeps, sleeps lightly, sleeps by me.
I must not watch him, and I must, as there he lies.
I must not watch too long, lest when he wakes, his eyes
Open to mine. I must not. It must not be.
I must watch instead the lizard or the tree,
Or the stones he knows so well: which recognize
The warm bright glance, affectionate and wise,
He turns upon them; so that I may not see
The sunlight fall on his mouth, nor the surrender
To sleep of his dark hair, nor clear and sweet
The curve of his silent cheek, the golden splendour
Of his throat and his arms and his thighs and his sandalled feet.
I will watch the lizard, or the stone, or the sky above him,
Lest he should see, when he wakes, dear Attilio, how dearly I
   love him.

———————————

She sleeps, Francesca sleeps, beside me, sleeps in grace.
I can see her how she is when I am away.
I can watch her as I have wanted to watch her all day.
And she will not know how well I know her face.
Secret her sleep. I am not there. All trace,
All thought of me is banished . . . I only stay
To be the first thing in her waking eyes; I only may
Protect till then that sleep in which I have no place.
Now I could hurt her, and will not; will not seek
To lay my hand softly on her soft breast;
I will not press my cheek against her cheek;
I will even her shining hair leave uncaressed;
I will not . . . I will only . . . oh, Francesca, can it do you harm,
If I place a kiss, like a whisper, into your open palm?

from *The Primal Scene, As It Were*

[SPERIAMO]

Under the moon
And the sweet-scented palms,
It was summer, and soon
You lay in my arms
And murmured so gently those sweet foreign words.
They sounded to me like the song of the birds . . .

Hasta la vista, you said, *je vous aime*.
I knew not the meaning, but I loved you the same.
Tre mila lire, you said, *s'il vous plaît*:
And I knew there was something stood in our way.

Yes, something was wrong then,
Between you and I,
And oh, I could see
From the look in your eye,
That *arrivederci*
Meant 'goodbye'.

ENGLISH LANE

There's many a place for a honeymoon tour
From Venice and Rome to Rocamadour,
There's the Costa Brava and Cap Ferrat,
Marrakesh and the Old Bazaar.
  But there's only one place for you and for I
  To watch the pageant of life go by;
  The only thing that will always remain
  Is the dear old sight of an English lane . . .

[*refrain*]
The gentle sigh of an English breeze
And rivers and hills and fields and trees

And sea and summer and air and sky
And clouds and cows as the days roll by.
  If I've said it before, let me say it again:
  The only place is an English lane.

I've loitered . . . in the streets of gay Vienna,
I've lingered . . . in palaces of old Siena,
I've waited . . . in a café in Montparnasse.
But what is there left when these things pass?
  The only thing that will always remain
  Is the dear old sight of an English lane.

[*refrain*]
Where English sun and clouds roll over
English sheep and English clover
And the scent of an English tree in leaf
And the honest taste of English beef.
  I have said it before and I say it again:
  The best place on earth is an English lane.

[*All*]
The gentle sigh of an English breeze
And rivers and hills and fields and trees
And sea and summer and air and sky
And clouds and cows as the days roll by.
  If I've said it before, let me say it again:
  The only place is an English lane.

PART V

Translations, Imitations
(1949–1975)

from the Italian of Giacomo Leopardi

CHORUS OF THE DEAD

And all returns to Thee, alone eternal,
And all to Thee returning.
Oh Death, in Thy vast shadow,
Simple and bare we languish,
Not happy, but from the anguish
Of life at last set free.
     The night profoundly
Falls on the shaken spirit,
And dark in dark confuses;
The withered soul courage and hope refuses;
Spent and uncaring,
Free now from sorrow and from fear for ever,
We lie here undespairing
Through slow eternity.
We lived . . .
    And as a phantom from a dream of terror
Wanders into the day,
And draws across the speechless souls of children
A memory and a fear,
We, as we linger here,
Are haunted still by life: but fears of children
Haunt us not now.
     What *were* we?
What was that bitter point in time
That bore the name of life?
Mysterious, stupendous,
Lost in our thought that hidden country lies:
As in our day of life there lay
The secret land of death. And as from dying
Our living souls drew back, so now they draw
Back from the flame of life,

Simple and bare to languish,
Not happy, but not in anguish;
For happiness we know
Fate upon life or death will not bestow.

[1949]

OH MISERO TORQUATO

. . . whom the sweet song
Comforted not, and could not melt the ice
Which secret hate and the foul tyrant's envy
Had set about your heart that once was warm; whom love,
The ultimate illusion of our life,
Abandoned. Nothingness for you
Was a real and solid shadow; and the world
Was an unpeopled shore.

(fragment) 1949

[AND TO THIS MEDITATION I SHALL BEAR]

. . . and to this meditation I shall bear
My idle days. Even in the sadness of truth,
There is delight. I speak of truth, and though
My words may in your ears discover neither
Welcome nor understanding . . . I shall not grieve.

In me the ancient, fair desire for fame
Lies spent already: goddess of vanity,
Blinder than fortune and fate, blinder than love.

(fragment) 1950 [1971]

THE INFINITE

Always to me beloved was this lonely hillside
And the hedgerow creeping over and always hiding
The distances, the horizon's furthest reaches.
But as I sit and gaze, there is an endless
Space still beyond, there is a more than mortal
Silence spread out to the last depth of peace,
Which in my thought I shape until my heart
Scarcely can hide a fear. And as the wind
Comes through the copses sighing to my ears,
The infinite silence and the passing voice
I must compare: remembering the seasons,
Quiet in dead eternity, and the present,
Living and sounding still. And into this
Immensity my thought sinks ever drowning,
And it is sweet to shipwreck in such a sea.

[1950]

TO HIMSELF

Here is your final rest.
I thought the last illusion would last for ever,
And it has perished. Perished, oh tired heart,
And now we know the loved illusion lost,
And after the dead hope, the dead desire.
Be still for ever. You
Have throbbed your fill. And nothing now
Is worth your trembling, earth is not worth your sighs.
Bitterness, vacancy
Is life, and nothing more, in a world of mire.
Lie here and rest. Let the despair that comes
Come finally. Fate never gave
To us, or any of us, more than a death. Now, here,
Curse if you will yourself and nature, curse the ways
Of the hidden ugly Power who orders our common ill,
And the infinite vanity of all our days.

[1950]

IMITATION

Far from the branch it blows,
The lost leaf, withering;
And ask it where it goes,
It answers: From the oak,
Where I grew, the wind has torn me
And turning, turning, has borne me
Out from the wood to the plain,
And I do not care to know
If to valley or hill it takes me.
I go where the wind makes me,
And care for no other thing.
I am lost to fear and grief,
I go to where all things go,
And I go in the natural way:
The way of the rose's petal,
And the way of the laurel's leaf.

[1950]

THE BROOM

or The Flower of the Desert

*And men chose darkness, even
when they were offered light.*
John 3: 19

So: here once more I find you
Happy in desert places; here where no other tree or flower
Gladdens the place, your scattered bushes grow
And on the air their scent and colour throw,
Oh sweet plantagenet,
Sweet-scented flower of the broom
Here you have made your home,
On the monstrous, barren ridge
Of this unpitying hill:
Vesévo: Vesuvius, the destroyer.
I find you here as once before I found you,
Your scattered bushes about the desert roads
Encircling Rome,
Who in her time was mistress of the world;
Even now, her empire gone,
Your flowers with their grave, unspeaking glance,
Bring memory of it, and belief in it,
To all who pass your way.
And here again I find you: still the lover
Of saddened places and abandoned worlds,
And still the comforter of afflicted fortunes.
Here you console
These slopes once more with barren ashes covered,
Once more with lava, once more turned to stone,
With the traveller's footsteps clinking over it.
The snake still nests and coils in the sun's heat,
The rabbit seeks its familiar hollow home.
Here once were revelling houses,
Here were fields
Ablaze with yellowing corn.
Here once were pastures
And murmuring herds upon them.
Gardens and palaces,

Restful for those with power
And wealth enough to rest.
And here you make your home,
Oh gentle flower; and
Pitying the fates of others, you
Address to heaven your sweetest scent as though
It might in some way plead for the wastes below.
And to these slopes,
Let him come boldly now whose wont it is
To praise men's state
Here let him see
How loving nature fondles the human race.
Here let him see and judge
How that harsh nurse covers her children's eyes.
When they least fear her, she
With one light gesture shakes away half their lives
And with another—scarcely a little stronger—
Grants them annihilation.
On these shores, full painted, let him see
Here of the human race
'The magnificent, progressive destiny'.

　　Here look, as in a glass,
Proud, foolish century:
The causeway to a new intelligence
Pointed before you: on this you turn your back.
You boast of your retreat,
And call it going forwards.
You are the guilty father of many sons,
Who praise your childish babblings to your face
And when you turn away, make you a laughingstock.
I am not of that race. I will not go
Down to my grave, laden with such disgrace.
Rather the great contempt I feel for you
Locked in my heart, I will some day release
When men shall ask me to.
Although I know
If we with our little world see too much sorrow
We court oblivion. And that oblivion
I shall share with you,

A fact which often makes me laugh.
You dream of freedom, and at the same time seek
To keep in bondage the thought that alone may raise us
A little above barbarity—and which alone
Can give us that civility which alone
Can better the fate of man.
This truth displeased you once:
The bitter lot, the despicable fate
Nature has willed on us. For that cause alone
You turned to darkness when you were offered that light.
And cravenly now,
You call him cowardly who follows it.
And greatness
Do you bestow only on the man
Who can laugh at his own and others' state
(Whether they are wise or fools)
And above the stars extols our human fate.

   A man in sickness and in poverty who
Still has a high and full-blooded heart will never
Boast himself rich or vigorous.
He will have the vision
To see how the world if he pretends to glory
Will hold him in derision.
And unashamed the man of honour lets the world
See him as feeble and poor
And says as much. He adds thereby
A little something to the world's small truth.
I have no trust, only contempt at best,
For the boasting animal fool
Who, born to perish, nourished on pain, will say
He was for joy created. He will fill
Page after page with his rank optimism
And promises of future happiness and bliss.
The heavens themselves are unaware of this,
And so are we. All we are promised here
Is the tidal wave, or the wind-borne plague,
Or the collapse of the earth beneath us.
These will destroy us, so completely that
Even memory may forget what we were like before.

The truly courageous race
With eyes they know will one day cease to see,
Still bear and bravely face
And still, fully and candidly,
The lowly, fragile and malignant state
We were all born to bear.
That man is honourable, who
Will declare his sufferings,
Nor add to them
The pains his fellow men inflict on him
(The worst that man can know)
Painful as these may be, he will not place
A blame for suffering on other men,
Who are his brothers, also in distress.
No: let him denounce
The real criminal who brought all men to birth,
And has become their evil foster mother,
Call her the enemy; and to combat her, know
All human beings must embrace each other
And stand in league against her; true love
Must be able and ready to give and accept itself
In the danger and agonies of our common war
Against the Giantess. We armed for the attack,
Let us not raise a hand against our comrades,
Or traps and pitfalls for our neighbours set,
Or act like one who knows himself beleaguered
Yet in the heat of battle can forget
There is an enemy,
And bitterly grow inflamed against his friends
And put them to flight, their swords
On one another turned.
Only when all men hold
Those truths as once they held them,
And all their horror against blasphemous Nature
That once united them shall be restored,
And helped a little by a deeper learning,
Will they return to truth
And the virtues of the honest citizen.
Justice and mercy will then have other roots
Than the imperious proud fooleries

That beguile a mob into the morality
It is used to bend to now.
It will find that truth is better based than error.

   Often on these sad shores,
I sit and watch the sombre clothes
That dress the stiffened flow of lava
Yet make it seem to move.
And over the gloomy waste,
I see on high out of the deepest blue
How flaming stars are mirrored far below
Sparkling and whirling in the distant sea,
A glittering world of happy emptiness.
I look above at those lights in the sky
And see them but as points. Yet they are immense
And to their gaze our earth and sea are merely
A tiny speck; and yes, indeed they are.
To them remain unknown
Not only man but the whole globe,
In which man counts for nothing.
And when I watch them,
So boundlessly remote, they mingle
And seem but a starry mist; and we to them
In all our number even with our golden sun
Must also seem only a space
Of nebulous light. Oh sons of men,
The soil I tread bears witness
How I should think of you
If I remember now your state on earth.
You have thought otherwise.
Have thought yourself the final aim of all.
You have even invented myths of how
The lords who made you have come down to you,
Upon this grain of sand we call the earth,
Their purpose merely a friendly chat with you.
When I consider
How in these frivolous dreams you insult the wise
Who to knowledge and civil behaviour have advanced us,
What feeling should I have, unhappy and mortal race?
I scarcely know whether to laugh or cry.

As from its tree a tiny apple falls
In full maturity falls and destroys
The happy dwelling place of a crowd of ants
Which they assiduously have hollowed out
In the soft earth and have stored therein
The whole of their wealth and riches
Laboriously collected in the summertime
To protect their winter . . . and now it is all destroyed
In a single moment.
Thus from her thunderous womb
The mountains flung on high
Her ruinous night,
Ashes, pumice, and rocks,
Which on the earth descended
To mingle with boiling streams
Bursting now from the gaping flanks
Of the mountain. The horrors met.
And together poured furiously through the fields
Rivers of molten metal,
Liquid and burning sand
Bringing immense distress
As they finally reached the sea and the cities,
Confounded them, broke them and straightway
Obliterated them.
    Yet over them now
Browses the goat. New towns arise
Founded upon the ruins of the old,
The tombs and buried walls.
The burning mount still has them at its feet.
Nature has as little care for the sons of men
As for the ant.
                    And if her carnage falls
More rarely upon the man than on the ant,
The reason can only be
Man breeds less rapidly.

    And eighteen hundred years
Have passed since the fiery power submerged
The populous places here.
                        And still the cottager

117

Tending his vines on this unhelpful soil
Still turns from time to time suspicious looks
Still fearful of the deadly height above him
Which nothing has ever tamed.
Terrible she sits there still, still threatening
Ruin to him and his, and their poor belongings.
Often the poor wretch lies at night in the open air
On the roof of his rustic home,
Sleepless, on guard, prompt to leap up and scan
The present course of the dreaded lava, pouring
Unceasingly down the sandy slopes
With a power enough to shed its glowing light
On the port of Naples and on Mergellina,
And even the beach of Capri.
And if he sees it nearing him, or if
He hears a riotous bubbling in his well,
He wakes his wife and children, and in haste
They flee straightway with what they may snatch up,
And watch from afar their dear familiar nest,
And the small field, their only sustenance,
Become a prey to the indifferent flow,
Grinding implacably onwards, arriving
To obliterate, once for all, their tiny home.
And now to the light of heaven returns
From underground the skeleton
Of dead Pompeii, disinterred
By avarice or piety
From underneath oblivion.
Here in the Forum's emptiness,
Erect the pilgrim stands between
The fallen colonnades and sees
From far away the smoking hill.
The cloven summit, threatening still
The shattered fragments of this place.
And threatening still:
Yes, in the horror of some still-hidden night,
Through ruined theatres and disfigured temples,
Through broken houses where only the bat now breeds,
Through empty palaces dismantled now,
You will once again flourish your bloody torch

And let the deadly lava's fiery stuff
Reach yet once more those quiet distances
Where we had thought you had already done harm enough.
Thus, unaware of man and of the ages
That he calls ancient, unaware
Of our succession: grandfather, father, son.
Nature is young forever: or rather,
She does go forward, but by so long a road,
She seems to be standing still. Meanwhile,
Kingdoms may fall, peoples and tongues may pass.
But this she does not observe:
And man boasts that eternity is his alone.

    And you, sweet flower of the broom
Slowly and sweetly spread
A ravishing scent across this ravished place
You too will yield with grace,
When the fiery power of the subterranean hell,
Returning once more to the place it knows so well,
Will nonchalantly spread its greedy flow
Over your modest blooms: and you will bow
Under the deadly weight your innocent head.
You will despise, as you have always done,
A craven pleading to the new oppressor.
And you will scorn to raise
A desperate pride upwards towards the stars
Even from this wilderness which
Was given you for your birthplace
Wiser than man, yet stronger,
Sweet flower of the broom, you have never
Believed that you, or your own offspring
Either by God's will or your own, would last forever.

1974

THE SETTING OF THE MOON

It is the same: the lonely night is on them,
Yet the moon still silvers the streams in the water-meadows
As the breeze caresses them;
And the lengthening shadows she sends from ever further away
Of tree and branch and hedge and garden and hill
Form and reform
And create on the gentle floor of the placid fields
Strange, always shifting, always deceptive scenes,
Unthinkable by day.
                        And the moon goes down.
At the remotest gates of the sky she must decline
Into the infinite womb of the Tyrrhene,
Or some far-distant Alp or Apennine
Will deprive the earth of her kindness.
                        The earth is drained of colour
There are no more shadows now: a single dark enshrouds
Valley and hill alike in the blind night's kingdom;
And on the road to home the tranter murmurs in song
The same goodbye he had sung to her as a greeting,
When in the whiteness of dawn she summoned him.
And the blind night sleeps on.

It is the same:
There is the setting of another moon: quicker: it takes from life
The days of youth and crumbles them into dust,
The promising delights betray their promise
Smaller, less often, come
The beguiling hopes our innocence took on trust.
Darkly, bereft, and wistfully,
Our life still clutches our hand. Straining his eyes,
In vain the bewildered traveller tries to see
In the long maze, whose ways he has to find,
Reason or scope.
                        He knows that something has gone;
That his place in the Future is something without hope,
And that the Future is indifferent to him.
She has never had him in mind.

It is as if they frowned on us from above,
Thinking us far too happy in this sad place.
(Do they know that our every good is only a payment for pain?)
They are alarmed that our youth may last forever.
They have pondered deeply on this. Death is too mild a fate:
And together they have devised something worse than our dread
   of death:
Something more terrible, something to meet on the road.

Oh, great Intelligence, who but you could enact
Triumphant as always, a crueller law than death?
And yet you have. You have invented *age*:
Age, painfullest of all, with hope expired and the fountains of
   pleasure dried,
All hardship growing harder, and respite all denied.
And only desire remaining: that you have left intact.

But you: oh, not for long, my dearest hills and beaches,
Will you be left deprived.
Never forever will ever the day's light leave you:
An hour or so, and you shall see the east
Quicken again: for you the sun will rise,
Hint after hint, until his whole light flames
And with his powerful flood,
Just as he bathes the heaven's ethereal fields,
Will bathe you too, flow over and retrieve you.
But for our human life,
When the grace of youth departs, there are no other dawns;
The dawns are gone forever; and in the night,
Which has shrugged countless ages out of sight,
The Gods have granted us one only casual light:
A white slab in the greenery of your lawns.

from the Greek of Theocritus

THE ENCHANTRESS

*SIMAETHA, a proud Syracusan lady, has been deserted by her lover,
 DELPHIS. In despair she resorts, at night, to sorcery to charm him back.*

Bring me the laurel leaves, oh bring them, bring them.
And bring the potion I must use against him.
Bring me the scarlet threads, that I may bind them
Around the bowl of flame, against the man I love,
Against you, oh Delphis, oh faithless one.

Twelve days have passed,
        And you, oh stony-hearted,
No longer can know
        Whether I live or die.
In their light hands
        Have love and Aphrodite
Borne off your heart
        By another's side to lie?

Go, then. Let them. I will enchant you back.

———————————

Oh moon, shine fair, I will murmur softly to you,
To you, bright Goddess of Heaven, to you, dark Goddess of
    Hell,
Hecate: black blood about you, whelps coursing round you,
Haunting death's places.

Dark Goddess, fill me, help me to the end.
Make now my spell as strong as the spell of Circe.
Give me the heart of Medea, give me the power
Of Perimede with the golden hair.

  Oh magic wheel, oh stay his footsteps,
  Draw hither to my house the man I love.

122

Now to the flames I fling you one by one. To the fire, to the fire!
Burn, barley-grains, burn as the bones of Delphis!
Burn, laurel-branch, burn as the flesh of his sides!
As the branch and the grain, may he be so consumed.

Oh magic wheel, oh stay his footsteps,
Draw hither to my house the man I love.

Dark Goddess, aid me: I melt the soft image of wax:
So let the heart of Delphis by love be melted.
Oh Aphrodite! I turn the restless wheel:
Thus let him turn, restless about my doors.

———————

Silent the sea, beneath the silent winds;
Only unsilent the knocking in my breast;
Silent the moon: ponder, oh moon, in silence:
Think of my love, oh holy moon, and whence it came.

How I saw him in the street among his companions,
How my heart went out to him, how I faltered there,
How I lay here, fevered and lost, for ten long days,
How I sent my slave-girl about the city to find him:
'Bid him come, bid Delphis come,
Bring him here, I am dying.'

How I heard his first footfall outside my door,
And the fire turned to ice in my veins,
And he entered, all golden and smiling, with garlands about him;
And he sat by my side, and he took my hand in his hand.

And he said: 'Simaetha, Simaetha.'
And he said: 'I could keep from you no longer.'
And he said: 'I was coming unsummoned, Simaetha.'
And he said: 'I have always loved you.'
And he said: 'Oh love, you have called me, oh love, you have
  saved me,

Have caught me from the fire of the longing that consumed me,
Oh love, I am here!
You have saved me from fire,' he said, 'from fire.'

———————————

And now in the fire I fling you, oh Delphis!
The barley, the laurel, the grain-husk, the snake, the venom,
The image of wax, and the scarlet fringe of your cloak:
It is you, oh Delphis, and I fling you to the flame!

Artemis, mover of all things, oh aid me . . . !
Listen: listen:
Through the deserted streets the dogs are baying!
The Goddess stands at the cross-roads!
Oh think, moon, of my love . . .

See, I am no longer laughed at, no longer mocked!
Companion or lover, he shall leave them,
He shall be mine again, shall lie in my arms again!
Our bodies, brighter than these flames, shall burn again together!
Oh magic wheel, enchanted fire!
I bless your power: and in your power I am answered.

[1951]

PART VI

Early poems, drafts and fragments
(1935–1986)

GREEN, SPLEEN, &c.: a sequence

GREEN

Dear, though the spring plays lightly with you now,
You must remember: Time will not roll back.
When thirty winters shall besiege your brow
And the little nymph be nymphomaniac,
Don't be surprised to see Love's ancient trick:
Your heaven sink further upward into sky,
Your little breasts to rise and fall more quick,
The valley deeper and the hills more high.
Open your arms again for my caresses,
Your haven where your ship of pleasure lies
Where mouth soothes mouth, and body body blesses
And pleasant ills have pleasant remedies.
    Ere Autumn whirl you to a worse newcomer
    Hold while you can, my Love, the shaking summer!

1937

SPLEEN

I do not love the lobster in your loins,
The butterflies that from your navel hiss,
Nor the great suction-pump that always joins
Its mouth to mine to intercept my kiss.
And when upon your gentle breasts I lie
(In due obedience to Nature's laws)
It is in truth iniquity on high
That they should open out in chests of drawers.
And when above you in the fields I bend,
With kindly forethought taking off my boots,
And, whispering, propose Love's right true end,
Your right true end is hid in mandrake-roots.
    Surrealist Love! For God's sake change your form
    Back to the splendours of the classic norm.

1937

127

One afternoon in Naples, the
large bright lady who was the
mother of Peppino, Vittorio
and Fernando leaned over to
me and said, *I am the nymph
Parthenope*; for apparently
Ulysses had appeared to her
in a vision and informed her
of the fact.

1935

FALANGE

Bilbao's fallen: clean your teeth, my Sweet,
Let my insurgent tongue come pressing forth,
And let your smiling regiments part to greet
Another rebel victory in the North.
Seville and Burgos are your shining breasts,
Held willing captives in my territory.
My men manoeuvre. And on both fair crests
There is a new cathedral, raised by me.
Why does Madrid then hold out for so long?
My five advancing armies know so well
Its garden suburbs (they are not so strong),
But its Red centre is a very Hell.
   Let no more Guadalajaras strike me dumb,
   But open: let your conquering Hero come!

1937

LYSISTRATA

And when we came home on Christmas
leave, our wives surprised us with
the impassioned greeting: Either
throw down those guns, or abjure
the pleasures of our beds! This
let us out nicely; for the pleasures
we had accustomed ourselves to in the
army had rendered the prospect of

Christmas leave that of an embarrassing
and boring interlude; and accordingly
we shall not sheathe the sword until
we have freed the smaller nations of
Europe from the perpetual and recurring
threat of German aggression.

1940

THE EUMENIDES

I am, as it happens, ana-
paranoiac, which is a word
I have collected together
myself: I mean that those
things which true paranoiacs
think pursue them really *do*
pursue me, and I take no
notice of them. They get
frightfully annoyed about it,
too.

1940

DULL SONNET

I have always been remarkably impressed
By the various sights and sounds of trees and birds
Respectively; have always thought that words
Could not express the beauties of the West
With much exactitude. Yet in my breast,
When pondering on the ruminating herds,
I have (not seldom) felt like one who girds
His spiritual loins; and have confessed
    That it is clear that those restrictive laws
    Which tie the tongues of men of meaner clay
    Do not apply to Me: that I have cause
    To assume, without compunction or delay,
    A just complacency, that scorns to hide
    In (a) mock modesty, or (b) false pride.

1939

DE ARTE POETICA

Shall these bones live again? And if they do,
How can they love this flesh they never knew?

I turn my hand to make the dead life live,
The fated, naked past again to thrive,

But the withered flower comes out with a different bloom,
The suffering ghost haunts in a strange room.

The words stream out, are fashioned into sense,
But not in the song I wished, this gross pretence,

Strange to my ear, false to my watchful eye;
I cannot live again, I can only die.

And if I choose one death to contemplate,
The rest break in, and fashion a new fate,

Fate that for good or ill was never mine,
Deaths whose mysterious source I can not divine.

The deaths I could now receive, they above all delay;
My unwished vengeance is that I betray

Even the wounds I have bled from. They are *here*:
Here is the spot, blanched with an ancient fear,

But under the visible line of the cicatrice
I am cured of a new disease, by a new device.

If I could show the simple dust as dust!
But murder replaces theft, greed is disclosed as lust;

Things I could wish at war are reconciled,
London becomes Rome, my father becomes my child.

How can the bones live? The bones are white and mute.
Here are my hands, but my hands are destitute

At once of the power to revive and the power to kill.
Here is a dull, white flower, solitary, simple, still:

I place it into a vase, with no thought or intent,
And therefore if I remark that by some accident

It stands in front of a mirror, the recognition soon
Goes from my mind, and mindlessly I pass the afternoon.

And only with half a consciousness am I aware at all,
How often the sun has flickered on, and vanished from, the
    wall,

And returned and withdrawn again, until at the evening hour
It advances its last full tide upon the inert flower.

There has only been the flower, and the flower's reflected nape,
The fragile white blossom, the slowly obscuring shape.

But into this unsought light the new ghosts softly break:
And I see the lit flower shining, white, palpable, opaque;

And there on the mirror's surface the day's young dust I see,
And beyond in the glass the flower again, but lit to translucency.

(And the flower still lingering there, faint and deprived of will,
The real, dull, dying flower, solitary, simple, still.)

And then, most ghostly of all, faintest and frailest and last,
High on the mirror's surface the flower's grey shadow is cast.

Time, age, and broken growth, the arranging hands of men,
Chance and the dulled ego, caught, lost, caught again,

And the whole transfigured net is thrown on the shores of fate,
Strange, stranded, yet briefly happy, happy in its strange state.

The dead bones inurned, the new ghosts mounting guard:
It is hard to traverse their presence, but not more hard

Than the fact that I cannot choose the words I would choose to
  say,
That I speak of yesterday's death, but never in a future way;

Though the only words of mine that I know could be believed
Need a future way of utterance which could only be achieved

If another language were mine, or another idiom or art
Would form in my mouth and stifle my used-up words at the
  start,

If I could seize from the future a sentence in which I was free
From the falsified recollection, the remembered falsity.

How shall the bones live? How shall the skeleton
Rise from the dead shore and across the sea press on,

Ignoring the port's noises, the sea, the indifferent birds;
How shall we go across, when our clumsy bundle of words

Is only a passport for shipwreck? A few yards out from land,
The familiar landmarks vanish, vanishes the well-known strand.

But the four ghosts round the mirror assemble and go before.
Day breaks, and finds us happy, but happy on a strange shore

With a nearby town murmuring, but murmuring in a foreign
  way,
Waking, and waking us to the life of a foreign day

In a land we may one day love, but a land we have not sought,
That grants us only the possession of thoughts we have not
  thought,

With the passport in our hand, faded and torn and stained,
And the journey's imagined wages eternally ungained.

THE FUTURE

How shall I one day be,
     Having no longer youth,
Nor power for ecstasy,
     Nor passion for truth,
     Nor even for uncouth
Pleasures of flesh and sense
     To drown me utterly?

Shall I wander along
     The streets with eccentric tread,
Admonishing the throng
     Or begging for bread,
     My eyes and heart dead
In a grimed body or face,
     Muttering a vile song?

I can go so far
     In my prophetic mind
To where my ears are
     Deaf, and my eyes blind
     And all my sense confined
To fears of heat and cold,
     And if I can go thus far

Then how can I not fear
     Lest I may one day be
A madman such as we hear
     Raving anonymously
     From a broken mind as he
Menaces the passing whores,
     Like Timon or Lear.

And how can I not as well
     Fear to become
One in that other hell:
     The wealthy home
     The bedizened living tomb
Of passions disavowed
     The marble shell

Of the world's coveted prize.
        Desires forgot,
Respected lust allowed,
        The rest not,
        And no disturbing thought
To lift in sudden shame
        The hand to cover the eyes.

Then how can I not pray
        That the image that stands between
Me and the future day
        Of that corrupted scene,
        How can I, who have seen
Your presence by my side
        Can I do else than pray

That this single profound
        Image that still could ring
My days with torment round
        May still be the good thing
        That teaches me to sing
And may in the end be that
        Which keeps me sound?

PSYCHOLOGICAL WARFARE

This above all remember: they will be very brave men,
And you will be facing them. You must not despise them.

I am, as you know, like all true professional soldiers,
A profoundly religious man: the true soldier has to be.
And I therefore believe the war will be over by Easter Monday.
But I must in fairness state that a number of my brother-officers,
No less religious than I, believe it will hold out till Whitsun.
Others, more on the agnostic side (and I do not contemn them)
Fancy the thing will drag on till August Bank Holiday.

Be that as it may, some time in the very near future,
We are to expect Invasion . . . and invasion not from the sea.
Vast numbers of troops will be dropped, probably from above,
Superbly equipped, determined and capable; and this above all,
Remember: they will be very brave men, and chosen as such.

You must not, of course, think I am praising them.
But what I have said is basically fundamental
To all I am about to reveal: the more so, since
Those of you that have not seen service overseas—
Which is the case with all of you, as it happens—this is the first
    time
You will have confronted them. My remarks are aimed
At preparing you for that.

                              Everyone, by the way, may smoke,
And be as relaxed as you can, like myself.
I shall wander among you as I talk and note your reactions.
Do not be nervous at this: this is a thing, after all,
We are all in together.

I want you to note in your notebooks, under ten separate
    headings,
The ten points I have to make, remembering always
That any single one of them may save your life. Is everyone
    ready?
Very well then.

                    The term, Psychological Warfare
Comes from the ancient Greek: psycho means character
And logical, of course, you all know. We did not have it
In the last conflict, the fourteen-eighteen affair,
Though I myself was through it from start to finish. (That is
    point one.)
I was, in fact, captured—or rather, I was taken prisoner—
In the Passchendaele show (a name you will all have heard of)
And in our captivity we had a close opportunity
(We were all pretty decently treated. I myself
Was a brigadier at the time: that is point two)
An opportunity I fancy I was the only one to appreciate
Of observing the psychiatry of our enemy
(The word in those days was always psychology,
A less exact description now largely abandoned). And though the
    subject
Is a highly complex one, I had, it was generally conceded,
A certain insight (I do not know how, but I have always, they
    say,
Had a certain insight) into the way the strangest things ebb up
From what psychoanalysts now refer to as the self-conscious.
It is possibly for this reason that I have been asked
To give you the gist of the thing, the—how shall I put it?—
The *gist*.

                    I was not of course captured alone
(Note that as point three) so that I also observed
Not only the enemy's behaviour; but ours. And gradually, I
    concluded
That we all of us have, whether we like it or lump it,
Our own individual psychiatry, given us, for better or worse,
By God Almighty. I say this reverently; you often find
These deeper themes of psychiatry crudely but well expressed
In common parlance. People say: 'We are all as God made us.'
And so they are. So are the enemy. And so are some of you.
This I in fact observed: point four. Not only the enemy
Had *their* psychiatry, but we, in a different sense,
Had ours. And I firmly believe you cannot (point six) master
Their psychiatry before you have got the gist of your own.

                              136

Let me explain more fully: I do not mean to imply
That any, or many, of you are actually mentally ill,
Though that is what the name would imply. But we, your
    officers,
Have to be aware that you, and many of your comrades,
May have a sudden psychiatry which, sometimes without
    warning,
May make you feel (and this is point five) a little bit odd.

I do not mean that in the sense of anything nasty:
I am not thinking of those chaps with their eyes always on each
    other
(Sometimes referred to as homosensualists
And easily detected by the way they lace up their boots)
But in the sense you may all feel a little disturbed,
Without knowing why, a little as if you were feeling an impulse,
Without knowing why: the term for this is ambivalence.
Often referred to for some mysterious reason,
By the professionals as Amby Valence,
As though they were referring to some nigger minstrel.
(Not, of course, that I have any colour prejudice:
After all, there are four excellent West Nigerians among you,
As black as your boot: they are not to blame for that.)

At all events this ambivalence is to be avoided.
Note that as point seven: I think you all know what I mean:
In the Holy Scriptures the word begins with an O,
Though in modern parlance it usually begins with an M.
You have most of you done it absentmindedly at some time or
    another,
But repeated, say, four times a day, it may become almost a
    habit,
Especially prone to by those of sedentary occupation,
By pale-faced clerks or schoolmasters, sitting all day at a desk,
Which is not, thank God, your position: you are always
More or less on the go: and that is what
(Again deep in the self-conscious) keeps you contented and
    happy here.

Even so, should you see some fellow-comrade
Behaving towards his person in a psychiatrical manner,

Give him all the help you can. In the spiritual sense, I mean,
With a sympathetic word or nudge, inform him in a manly
    fashion
'Such things are for boys, not men, lad.'
Everyone, eyes front!

                    I pause, gentlemen.
I pause. I am not easily shocked or taken aback,
But even while I have been speaking of this serious subject
I observe that one of you has had the effrontery —
Yes, you at the end of row three! No! Don't stand up, for God's
    sake, man,
And don't attempt to explain. Just tuck it away,
And try to behave like a man. Report to me
At eighteen hundred hours. The rest of you all eyes front.
I proceed to point six.

                    The enemy itself,
I have reason to know is greatly prone to such actions.
It is something we must learn to exploit: an explanation, I think,
Is that they are, by and large, undeveloped children,
Or adolescents, at most. It is perhaps to do with physique,
And we cannot and must not ignore their physique as such.
(Physique, of course, being much the same as psychiatry.)
They are usually blond, and often extremely well-made,
With large blue eyes and very white teeth,
And as a rule hairless chests, and very smooth, muscular thighs,
And extremely healthy complexions, especially when slightly
    sunburnt.
I am convinced there is something in all this that counts for
    something.
Something probably deep in the self-conscious of all of them.
Undeveloped children, I have said, and like children,
As those of you with families will know,
They are sometimes very aggressive, even the gentlest of them.

All the same we must not exaggerate; in the words of Saint
    Matthew:
'Clear your minds of cant.' That is point five: note it down.
Do not take any notice of claptrap in the press

                            138

Especially the kind that implies that the enemy will come here,
Solely with the intention of raping your sisters.
I do not know why it is always sisters they harp on:
I fancy it must ebb up from someone's self-conscious.
It is a patent absurdity for two simple reasons: (a)
They cannot know in advance what your sisters are like:
And (b) some of you have no sisters. Let that be the end of that.

There are much darker things than that we have to think of.
It is you they consider the enemy, you they are after.
And though, as Britishers, you will not be disposed to shoot
   down
A group of helpless men descending from the heavens,
Do not expect from them—and I am afraid I have to say
   this—gratitude:
They are bound to be over-excited,
As I said, adolescently aggressive, possibly drugged,
And later, in a macabre way, grotesquely playful.
Try to avoid being playfully kicked in the crutch,
Which quite apart from any temporary discomfort,
May lead to a hernia. I do not know why you should laugh.
I once had a friend who, not due to enemy action
But to a single loud sneeze, entirely his own, developed a hernia,
And had to have great removals, though only recently married.
(I am sorry, gentlemen, but anyone who finds such things funny
Ought to suffer them and see. You deserve the chance to.
I must ask you all to extinguish your cigarettes.)

There are other unpleasant things they may face you with.
You may, as I did in the fourteen-eighteen thing,
Find them cruelly, ruthlessly, starkly obsessed with the arts,
Music and painting, sculpture and the writing of verses,
Please, do not stand for that.

                    Our information is
That the enemy has no such rules, though of course they may
   have.
We must see what they say when they come. There can, of
   course,
Be no objection to the more virile arts:

139

In fact in private life I am very fond of the ballet,
Whose athleticism, manliness and sense of danger
Is open to all of us to admire. We had a ballet-dancer
In the last mob but three, as you have doubtless heard.
He was cruelly teased and laughed at—until he was seen in the
  gym.
And then, my goodness me! I was reminded of the sublime story
Of Samson, rending the veil of the Temple.
I do not mean he fetched the place actually *down*; though he
  clearly did what he could.
Though for some other reason I was never quite clear about,
And in spite of my own strong pressure on the poor lad's behalf,
And his own almost pathetic desire to stay on with us,
He was, in fact, demobilized after only three weeks' service,
Two and a half weeks of which he spent in prison.
Such are war's tragedies: how often we come upon them!
(Everyone may smoke again, those that wish.)

This brings me to my final point about the psychiatry
Of our formidable foe. To cope with it,
I know of nothing better than the sublime words of Saint Paul
In one of his well-known letters to the Corinthians:
'This above all, to thine own self be true,
And it must follow, as the night the day
No man can take thee in.'

'This above all': what resonant words those are!
They lead me to point nine, which is a thing
I may have a special thing about, but if so,
Remember this is not the first war I have been through.
I refer (point nine this is) to the question of dignity.
Dignity. Human dignity. Yours. Never forget it, men.
Let it sink deep into your self-consciousness,
While still remaining plentifully available on the surface,
In the form of manly politeness. I mean, in particular, this:
Never behave in a manner to evoke contempt
Before thine enemy. Our enemy, I should say.

                    Comrades, and brothers-in-arms,
And those especially who have not understood my words,

You were not born to live like cowards or cravens:
Let me exhort you: never, whatever lies you have heard,
Be content to throw your arms on the ground and your other
    arms into the air and squawk '*Kaputt!*'
It is unsoldierly, unwarlike, vulgar, and out of date,
And *may* make the enemy laugh. They have a keen sense of
    humour,
Almost (though never quite, of course) as keen as our own.
No: when you come face to face with the foe, remember dignity,
And though a number of them do fortunately speak English,
Say, proudly, with cold politeness, in the visitor's own language:
'*Ich ergebe mich.*' *Ich* meaning I,
Ergebe meaning surrender, and *mich* meaning me.
'Ich ergebe mich.' Do not forget the phrase.
Practise it among yourselves: do not let it sound stilted,
Make it sound idiotish, as if you were always saying it,
Only always cold in tone: icy, if necessary:
It is such behaviour that will make them accord you
The same respect that they accorded myself,
At Passchendaele. (Incidentally,
You may also add the word *nicht* if you feel inclined to,
Nicht meaning not. It will amount to much the same thing.)

Dignity, then, and respect: those are the final aims
Of psychiatric relations, and psychological warfare.
They are the fundamentals also of our religion.
I may have mentioned my own religious intuitions:
They are why I venture to think this terrible war will be over
On Easter Monday, and that the invasion will take place
On either Maundy Thursday or Good Friday,
Probably the Thursday, which in so very many
Of our great, brave, proud, heroic and battered cities,
Is early closing day, as the enemy may have learnt from their
    agents.
Alas, there may be many such days in the immediate future.
But remember this in the better world we all have to build,
And build by ourselves alone—for the government
May well in the next few weeks have withdrawn to Canada—
What did you say? The man in row five. He said something.
Stand up and repeat what you said.

I said 'And a sodding good job', sir, I said, sir.
I have not asked anyone for political comments, thank you,
However apt. Sit down. I was saying:
That in the better world we all have to try to build
After the war is over, whether we win or lose,
Or whether we all agree to call it a draw,
We shall have to try our utmost to get used to each other,
To live together with dignity and respect.
As our Lord sublimely said in one of his weekly Sermons on the
   Mount
Outside Jerusalem (where interestingly enough,
I was stationed myself for three months in 1926):
'A thirteenth commandment I give you (this is point ten)
That ye love one another.' Love, in Biblical terms,
Meaning of course not quite what it means today,
But precisely what I have called dignity and respect.
And that, men, is the great psychiatrical problem before you:
Of how on God's earth we shall ever learn to attain some sort
Of dignity.
                    And due respect.
                              One man.
                                        For another.
Thank you; God bless you, men. Good afternoon.

THE CHÂTEAU

Yet will I fear no evil: not even here.
Nor even now.
                    Now, at the ending of the autumn afternoon,
And here, on the wide stone terrace confronting the great
    château,
The enormous flagstones with the small, scattered tables,
Where a few of us sit, apart from each other, indifferent.
(Yet I am not indifferent, I am most dearly concerned)

There are not many of us. We face the great grey mansion
Whose doors and windows glare back at the sunless light,
And from the high flagpoles the long pennants, unenflamed,
Droop into the colourless day.
                    Is some great Someone here,
For whom these pennants hang? There is no one to ask.
And one might be too frightened to ask.
                    Yet will I fear no evil,
Not even here or now.

For surely beyond that great façade my life is being lived?
Lived, loved and filled with gaiety and ardour,
As though my life were endowed with a perpetual splendour
And radiance fell on it. It is surely only that I
Am not now with it, not with my life, but here,
Restlessly rigid, counting the flagstones while there within,
    it dances
Nightly the length of the lighted hall to the starry feast,
Stoops in the dawn to the kindly fountain, rests and, rested,
Breathes on a single breath its anthem of love and praise.

Surely there will be a signal? Inconspicuously,
One of the giant roses in the gardens around us
Will perhaps explode on to the autumn grass:
Something like that, perhaps. I know I shall know the moment.

And surely (and almost now) it will happen, and tell me
That now I must rise and with firm footsteps tread
Across the enormous flagstones, reach, find and know
My own and veritable door;

143

I shall open it, enter, and learn
That in all this hungry time I have never wanted,
But have, elsewhere, on honey and milk been fed,
Have in green pastures somewhere lain, and in the mornings,
Somewhere beside still waters have
Mysteriously, ecstatically, been led.

A GOOD DREAM

... And for some reason I said, 'I will not go.'
It was a park or a garden, hilly and green,
And a flight of birds from a Roman portico
Flew out and under with a sudden brush of wings,
Small birds on heavy wings, and they swept out
As it might be pigeons or doves into an air
Suddenly summer again, and I saw that my arms were bare
And brown once more and that was good again,
And a duty nagged at my forehead, but in that air
Suddenly I knew from somewhere I did not care.
I forget if I wept as I said it, but if so,
It was the duty weeping, not I, and in fact
I do not think I wept at all, I was not in pain,
For something in that blithe air no longer mattered
And something that had been broken was now intact,
And I said, 'Why should I go?' or 'I need not go',
And the vanishing birds and embowered air gave me to know
That I was free of something and need not go ...

THE INTRUDER

I

There were ten days of absence
In other places I knew
And then I came back by water
Back up the sliding coast
Of creek and cavern and harbour
Hillside to leeward curving
And landward the same things shone
Viewless, but known as there:
As tamarisk, pine and pine-cone,
Pine-needle and pine by rock
And leaf of olive, and shining
Sail against shining sky
And the shining waters there

Your sea that changes only
In aspects of eternal sameness,
That sea, your sea, not mine:
The sweeping flight of fishes
Swerving in the long blue swell
The porpoises leaping over
And deeply the red reefs under
With their green scarves sombrely always
Swaying in the long blue swell
Tossing and waving and weaving
Under the flickering waters
Of that sea, your sea, not mine.

II

But even as you embraced me
Even as among the greetings
Of others who embraced,
My strangers, your familiars,
Who did not regard us as lovers
(As we were not, and were never)
I saw, as you did not see
My heart against yours reunited,

Your passionate kiss on my cheek,
I saw, to still my pleasure,
Saw him, for the first time showing,
Saw there my noonday ghost
Pleading with me, and asking
Something I could not answer,
The spectre of one who seemed
Seeking and seeking and seeking
Something I dared not say,
And bent in distress beside me
Ashen and anguished and lonely.

III

And as we paced the quayside
And on up the sunlit hill,
Your hill, and almost mine,
So familiar the houses,
The tamarisk, pine and pine-cone
And the shining leaf of olive
As if they would never alter
Never be other than ours,
He was there beside us, or
At the other side of you, or
Holding my other arm, or
Walking towards us and trying
To meet us and greet us and
Trying to do us no harm, but
Still not even between us
I saw that whenever you spoke,
He would try to answer before me.

IV

His was an agèd face,
Lined with beseeching pathos,
The agèd hands, pigmented with curious freckles,
    brushed
From the agèd body's clothing
Imaginary dust or ash
As though to regain some pride,

147

Some antique jauntiness
And I saw he was visiting again this place
A quarter-century hence
And pausing and hoping and sighing,
Recapturing a half or a third
Of what we were saying there now,
As though what we said had mattered,
There by the base of the fountain
Or at that pause on the hill-side
Where we always said our goodbyes

Day in day out through that summer
Of shining pine-cone and pine,
Where we always said our goodbyes,
He followed and placed one hand
Against his forehead and tried
Unassuageably, to remember something.
Or, one hand joined to the other
He would cover his face with his hands
—What was he trying, there in the sunlight, to rememb
Who our bright friends had been
Or to solve and establish the moment
Where and when we had first spoken
(I forget myself the moment)
And where we had first embraced
(And you have forgotten it also)
But to him it was all-important.
And where we had first accepted
The end of our first season
We, the ephemera
Burnt on the breeze, blown on the zephyr,
Floating upon the wind

Tamarisk, pine and pine-cone
Pine-needle, and pine by rock,
Leaf of the olive and shining
Sail against shining sky

As seen and seen for always
The bright white curve of the hill-side
Where I would bid you goodbye
And turn to wave you goodbye
As I descended alone
And as I turned you were there
As always you were waiting and daring
The other to disappear

And there I turned to wave
And turned again and there
Alone in the beating sunlight
There stood he, he stood there
Not waving, not weeping, but there.

THE SOUND OF HORSES' HOOVES

And this had all the signs of permanence.
  For centuries the headlong rush of beauty
Had sought, and here had found, alighting gently
  A face it could rest on fully, breathing, elated,
Then, with a long calm, nestling there, contented.
  A face to move me, suddenly to tears,
  It could have settled in my heart for years.
And in a minute I had forgotten it.

At the café-table, under the low soft pines,
  Green light about us, not far from the tragic music,
And the sea not far away either, there did I see you
  I watched you, but not for long.
I dropped my gaze to my book, to the muted torment
  There on the page. The scene, high up in the mountains.
A custom-house near a frontier. Politics. A private man
  Retired to himself, absorbed with a silent grief
Whose nature, unconfessed, eluded others,
  And ate unpityingly away his years.
  I raised my eyes again to think of it.
Had you been gone when I did so, what then? Would I have felt
  At the sight of an empty chair a loss
Greater than the possession that was mine again as I saw you,
  Or would you have been forgotten, lost entirely,
As countless others have been lost in such conditions,
  When a different world, captured in words, will rise and
      dismiss
This world of our own, our world that moves
  In minutes unrecorded and incomplete?

  Did you, in your turn, in those moments while I forgot you
Wonder what so possessed a stranger's bending head,
  That he could ignore the sunlit day, and exchange it,
Exchange the music and the shining harbour?
  How could you guess, or if you guessed
That in my long first look, I had known I could put
  The thoughts of all my days and nights around you
How could you further guess that in a second

I could feel all that, and in another second
Could forget you and lose you forever.

But you were there, after all; you were gently smiling towards
    me.
And so it chanced that I looked up again
    And our eyes met. You smiled and astoundingly said
'Allow me to mention it, sir, we are reading the same book.'
    You held up your copy to prove this.
'Why so we are,' I faltered. 'In that case perhaps you will help
    me.'
    'Certainly, if I can. Is there something
You do not understand?' 'I was wondering,' I said,
    'What is the meaning of the word *scalpiccio*?'
'It is not a common word, certainly,' you said,
    'But it means the sound of horses' hooves, trampling or
        stamping.'

'Ah, it is that,' I said. 'Somehow I thought it might mean
    The sound of horses' hooves, but I see that it cannot be that.'
'No, not quite that: though a similar word, *scalpitio*,
    Means the pawing of horses' hooves on the ground.'
('Printing their proud hooves i' the receiving earth', I thought
    And dismissed the thought.) Oh, how to express
The ecstatic peace that began to invade my heart
As you spoke, as you smiled and spoke. No gesture
    Attended your speech. Your one hand still held your book,
A finger hooked in it, and the other lay quietly unmoved
    On the seat beside you. Spellbound I watched you.
I was conscious of being looked at and spoken to
    And of attempting to answer. We had talked for a minute.
We had been strangers, before that minute, and now
    Would never till the end of time be strangers again.
Thus the magic began. Words, but no gestures.
    We spoke. We spoke of our author, his gift, and his recent
        death
Premature, as these things go. We spoke
    Of the open-air theatre in the graveyard across the bay.
The players in *Romeo*, the peals of hilarious laughter
    As a row of children sitting on the graveyard wall

Heard Juliet declaim her terrible apprehension
    Of waking in the tomb wherein cold Tybalt lay
(The director had been much moved by this, I was able to tell
        you).
    We talked. At times we paused—when the tragic music
        paused,
Or a waiter brought us wine—and we each had the chance
    Of testing the quality of each other's silences,
And of how our silences mingled. There was nothing amiss.
    We paused to watch and admire a valorous harbour-boy
Who had climbed on the harbour-wall to rehearse and display
    His elegant slow cart-wheels along the rough stone ledge.

Not at a loss for words. We spoke of the contentment
    Of speaking another language, the charms of another
        grammar,
We spoke of the delights of the place we were in.
    The green light around us changed a little
As the afternoon moved towards evening.
    We did not intently inspect each other,
Not even furtively. There was nothing we had to learn.
    We had from time to time met directly each other's eyes
In passing, as it were.

The gentle, eager young man who had to sell postcards
    Paused nearby, waiting for us to fall silent
Before advancing to offer us his gleaming images.
    We bought two apiece, and spoke to him of their beauty.

Then we resumed our discourse with one another
    And our silences with each other [. . .]

THE VOW

You are the only vow I keep,
A name I do not name, an oath
I will not take, but shall not break,
Which comes as though demanding faith
In sleep, or on the ledge of sleep
Admonishing me: 'Never weep.'
You are the only vow I keep,
And though the clouds of faithlessness
Sprawl over the brief, unyielding day
And over the thin dishevelled street
And over me, who always may
The trusts of other skies betray,
You are the only vow I keep,
Still and forever watching me.
As from a cave of lies I creep,
Dragging a sour profanity,
You call from silence: 'Care for me,'
As if I might not.
   As if I might not.
You are the only vow I keep,
And still in some untarnished place,
Like a small echo in my soul,
As I awake from threatening dreams.
Are always there, that I may catch,
Even through days of destined hell,
The five notes of its distant bell,
Telling me: 'All may yet be well.'

[L'ENVOI]

They told him, with reassurance: 'You must turn over a new
    leaf.'
Ever submissive and grateful, he did so and then said: 'Look!
This brings me to the last page in the book.
And the pages have been so thin I can clearly see
The earlier words that a week ago were me.'
He explains this simple fact. And they agree.
'Then tear the whole sheet out. Why not?' They do not see
That this would only show, naked, the pages before
Which he would most wish to efface,
To forget even more
Than this latest, dreadful page, as it seemed to him, of disgrace.

Then 'Buy a completely new book then,' they said, 'and burn the
    old.'
'Yes, that's an idea,' he said. And as they watched the flames
Slowly and gladly consume the crowded sheets
They were cheerful at least. It even relieved the cold
That had long crept in from the pitiful, pitiless streets.

'And buy it at once. Start now,' encouraging they said.
'I will,' he said, and moved to the window, looked out.
They warmed their hands at the blaze,
Glad he would start again, glad of their wisdom.
'Get a new book, and start at once,' they had said,
'And you will have, as you once did, happy days.'
He said, 'It is Sunday. And snowing like hell. And the shops are
    shut.'
They smiled indulgently and beckoned him to the fire. He
    returned and sat down to rest.
'There is always Monday,' they said. 'Yes, and Tuesday and
    Wednesday,' he added,
'Though Thursday is half-day closing,' he murmured, sighing
And a shiver ran over the room as some of them guessed
The last page had been the last and on Friday
Or possibly Saturday he would be dying.

NOTES

INDEX OF FIRST LINES

NOTES
Textual and Bibliographical

(HR = Henry Reed)

Dates in square brackets following the poems denote first publication.

PART I from *A Map of Verona* (1946, 1947)

Text from *A Map of Verona* / Poems by Henry Reed / London: Jonathan Cape, 1946 / 60 pp., except for those items marked *, which appear only in the US edition, *A Map of Verona and other poems* / New York: Reynal & Hitchcock, 1947 / 92 pp., containing additional poems and Notes by the author. Both editions are dedicated to Michael Ramsbotham.

PRELUDES

THE DESERT

     HR's note in the New York edition of *A Map of Verona* (p. 91):

     The passages containing the lines 'What do these comings and goings
     profit me' [l. 90] and 'If I am in your debt, to whatever degree' [l. 122] are
     partly adapted from letters written by Rimbaud in his later years. The
     former of these was sent to his mother while Rimbaud was living in
     Abyssinia; and the idea of Rimbaud's sojourn there was one of the things
     that helped to shape this poem in my mind.   23

TINTAGEL

HR's note on the sequence in the New York edition:

These poems were provoked by a visit to the actual ruins of Tintagel
Castle in Cornwall, though they were written at periods long separated
from each other. They represent four aspects of a problem known in one
or more of these aspects to most men and women. The incident in the
third of them, and the phrase 'the golden lie' [l. 46], come from Godfrey
of Strasbourg's version of the Tristram story.

TRIPTYCH

Of the three poems in the group so titled in the New York edition, only
'Chrysothemis' and 'Philoctetes' appear in the London edition of 1946. HR's
note in the New York edition:

These three poems, which are spoken respectively at sunset, nighttime
and day-break, centre on three characters from Sophocles: taken
together, they represent a moral progression, culminating in a decision.
The first is about Chrysothemis, the passive, evasive sister of Electra and
Orestes; the children referred to are the children of Clytemnestra and
Aegisthus. The second is a dialogue between two onlookers who have
been disturbed by the events concerning Antigone and her self-sacrifice
on behalf of her brother Polynices. The third is spoken by Philoctetes on
the morning after his decision to return and use his human
persuasiveness on Neoptolemus, partly by the more or less divine
injunction of Hercules. The poems were intended to form a whole; but
'Antigone' was finished after the others, and is not included in the English
edition of this book.

CHRYSOTHEMIS (first published, *New Writing and Daylight*, Winter
  1942–3; reprinted, *Penguin New Writing* no. 26, 1945).   37
*ANTIGONE (*Penguin New Writing* no. 30, 1947)   40
PHILOCTETES (*New Writing and Daylight*, Autumn 1944)   43

PART II *Lessons of the War* (1946, 1970)

Text from *Lessons of the War*, limited edition / London and New York:
Clover Hill Editions, 1970 / 35 pp., which reprints nos. 1, 2 and 4 from *A
Map of Verona* (1946, 1947), with the two later poems, nos. 3 and 5. The
dedication to Alan Michell of the sequence 'Lessons of the War' in *A Map of
Verona* is preserved in the 1970 limited edition.

1 NAMING OF PARTS (first published, *New Statesman and Nation*, 8
  August 1942); collected as 'Lessons of the War' I, *A Map of Verona*)   49
2 JUDGING DISTANCES (first published, *New Statesman and Nation*, 6
  March 1943); collected as 'Lessons of the War' II, *A Map of Verona*)   50
3 MOVEMENT OF BODIES (first published, *Listener*, 6 April 1950). A
  typescript among the author's papers contains an autograph
  emendation evidently made after the Clover Hill text was published; it
  alters the last line of stanza 11 from 'Yesterday a man was sick' to the
  reading given here.   52
4 UNARMED COMBAT (first published, *New Statesman and Nation*, 28
  April 1945; collected as 'Lessons of the War' III, *A Map of Verona*)   55
5 RETURNING OF ISSUE (first published, *Listener*, 29 October 1970). The
  1970 Clover Hill Editions text has substantive variants from that
  published in the *Listener*, notably the brackets introduced in stanzas 1,
  2, 4, 12, 13, 15 and 16 to give an antiphonal effect not so signalled in
  the earlier version.   57

PART III Uncollected poems (1950–1975)

THE CHANGELING (first published, *Listener*, 19 January 1950).   63
AUBADE (first published, *A Garland for the Queen*, London: Stainer & Bell,
  1953); one of a group of modern madrigals set by Sir Arthur Bliss for
  the 1953 Coronation of Queen Elizabeth II.   65
THE AUCTION SALE (*Encounter*, October 1956). Broadcast, BBC Third
  Programme, 20 September 1958. The text reproduced here incorporates
  HR's autograph emendations on a cutting, found among his papers, of the
  poem as reprinted in the magazine *Lot One*, July 1983. In *Who's Who* for
  1977 HR listed among his publications a volume entitled *The Auction Sale
  and Other Poems* (1977), but no such collection ever appeared.   66
THE INTERVAL (*Listener*, 27 November 1969). Both a *Listener* cutting
  among the author's papers and a fair copy inscribed to John Tydeman,
  probably from a later date, contain autograph emendations reflected in the
  text reproduced here.   74
THE RIVER (*Listener*, 26 March 1970); 'a separate silence' (l. 21) and 'to
  become the one who' (l. 22) reproduce autograph alterations made in HR's
  hand on a cutting of the text as printed in the *Listener*.   76

PART IV From the radio plays (1947–1979)

from *Moby Dick* (1947, 1979)

First broadcast, BBC Third Programme, 26 January 1947; published the same year, as *Moby Dick: A Play for Radio from Herman Melville's Novel* (London: Jonathan Cape, 1947). Five verse excerpts published (as 'Ishmael' I–V) in the US edition of *A Map of Verona* (New York, 1947), with a Note by the author. New BBC Radio 3 production by John Tydeman, first broadcast 2 February 1979, in a revised version with a new Epilogue.

'If you touch at the islands' (published as 'Ishmael' I, *A Map of Verona*, New York, 1947). HR's note (p. 92 in the New York *Map*) refers to the five passages excerpted there as 'lyric interludes'; in the radio play the lines are spoken antiphonally by Ishmael and Father Mapple.

'Whiteness is lovely' (as 'Ishmael' II, *A Map of Verona*, New York, 1947). The passage, as HR noted in the New York *Map*, 'is a brief paraphrase of the chapter in [Melville's] novel called "The Whiteness of the Whale" '.

[Cabaco's song] 'The white-walled town is far away' (*Moby Dick: A Play for Radio*, 1947; reprinted, *Music and Letters*, October 1953)

'Can you think what that life is like' (as 'Ishmael' III, *A Map of Verona*, New York, 1947)

'Oh, higher than albatross soaring' (as 'Ishmael' IV, *A Map of Verona*, New York, 1947)

'We are hunting a white whale' (as 'Ishmael' V, *A Map of Verona*, New York, 1947). Both 'Ishmael' IV and V also contain echoes of Melville's prose, as HR noted in New York 1947 *Map*.

[Ishmael's epilogue] 'No, you are gone, oh King' (revised ending to the 1979 BBC production; unpublished). In his Preface to the published *Moby Dick: A Play for Radio* (1947), HR had written: '... The destruction of Ishmael with the rest of the crew is the only deliberate falsification of the story I have permitted myself . . . Melville puts into his mouth an epilogue with a beautiful last sentence: it was there to be used if I wished. But these lines, which are not an anticlimax in the book, run the risk of being so on the air . . .' For the 1979 radio version HR apparently changed his mind: Ishmael is allowed to live, and his final speech reproduced here is perhaps the last extended piece of verse Henry Reed completed. The text is from a carbon of his autograph fair copy, dated 6 January 1979 and inscribed to the actor Philip Scully, who played Ishmael in the 1979 production; the carbon was found among HR's papers.   89–94

from *Pytheas* (1947)
    First broadcast (as *Pytheas: A Dramatic Speculation*), BBC Third Programme, 25 May 1947; unpublished. The text of a song and four speeches in verse are from a carbon typescript, containing autograph emendations, preserved among the author's papers.   95–99

Published in *The Streets of Pompeii and Other Plays for Radio* (London: BBC Publications, 1971):
    'Little bird, my little dove' (from *The Monument*, first broadcast, BBC
        Third Programme, 7 March 1950; published as *Leopardi* / Part Two)
    [Shakespeare's lullaby] 'Sing lullaby, as women do' (from *The Great Desire
        I Had*, first broadcast [with the subtitle *Shakespeare and Italy*], BBC
        Third Programme, 26 October 1952)
    [Francesca and Attilio] 'He sleeps, Attilio sleeps' (from *The Streets of
        Pompeii*, first broadcast, BBC Third Programme, 16 March 1952, and
        in a new production, 22 April 1955)   100–102

Published in *Hilda Tablet and Others: Four Pieces for Radio* (London: BBC Publications, 1971):
    [*Speriamo*] 'Under the moon / And the sweet-scented palms'
    English Lane (both from *The Primal Scene, As It Were*, first broadcast
        [with the subtitle *Nine Studies in Disloyalty*] 11 March 1958, with music
        by Donald Swann)   103

PART V Translations, Imitations (1949–1975)

from the Italian of Giacomo Leopardi (1798–1837):

CHORUS OF THE DEAD (*Coro di Morti*, from 'Dialogo di Federico Ruysch
    e delle sue Mummie', *Operette Morali*); broadcast 6 February 1949, BBC
    Third Programme, in 'Brief Moralities: Three Dialogues from Leopardi's
    Operetti Morali'; and 12 January 1975 in 'An Essential Voice' (anthology
    of Leopardi); first published, *Listener*, 28 April 1949.   107

OH MISERO TORQUATO (fragment from *Canti* III, 'Ad Angelo mai'):
    broadcast 6 February 1949, in 'Brief Moralities' (as above); unpublished.
    Text from carbon typescript with autograph emendations, preserved
    among the author's papers.   108

'. . . and to this meditation I shall bear' (fragment, after Leopardi, 'Al Conte Carlo Pepoli', *Canti* XIX); spoken by HR's character Leopardi in the radio play *The Monument*, first broadcast 7 March 1950; published in *The Streets of Pompeii* (London: BBC Publications, 1971). 108

THE INFINITE (*L'infinito*), broadcast 12 January 1975 in 'An Essential Voice'; first published *Listener*, 25 May 1950. 109

TO HIMSELF (*A se stesso*), broadcast 12 January 1975 in 'An Essential Voice'; first published, *Listener*, 1 June 1950. Cf. Leopardi's lines in *The Monument* (*Streets of Pompeii*, p. 111), 'Oh hidden ugly Power that orders our common ill', for an echo of line 15 of this poem. 110

IMITATION (*Imitazione*), first published, *Listener*, 15 June 1950, with the acknowledgement 'From the French of Arnauld and the Italian of Leopardi'. The double attribution is exact: Leopardi's 'Imitazione', composed *c.*1818 but published only after his death, is a version of the lament 'La Feuille', by Antoine-Vincent Arnauld (1766–1834), written a few days before leaving France to go into exile under the Second Restoration. In Leopardi's version banishment is given a wider application, and the oak leaf torn from the branch is left to wander all of nature, not just the world outside monarchist France. 111

THE BROOM, or The Flower of the Desert (*La Ginestra o il fiore del deserto*), broadcast 12 January 1975 in 'An Essential Voice'. The lines 'You dream of freedom . . . /. . . and the world's small truth' (ll. 72–97 of the original) were omitted from the broadcast version (or from the BBC transcript of the broadcast, which is the basis for the present text), and are here supplied from HR's undated early drafts of the translation, kept among his papers. He seems to have been occupied with versions of this famous poem (always by him entitled 'The Plantagenet') from the beginning of the 1950s, and the choruses of the Sibyl in the radio play *The Streets of Pompeii* (first broadcast 1952, published 1971) echo many lines from the translation apparently not completed until *c.*1974, and until now unpublished. 112

THE SETTING OF THE MOON (*Il tramonto della luna*); unpublished. The version reproduced here is from a fair copy sent to Hallam Tennyson with a letter dated 22 September 1975, in which HR noted:

> One odd point: the word 'imbruna' [l. 14 in the original]. It means, of course, darkens, since 'bruno' is rarely, if ever, used in Italian to mean 'brown' . . .. But I originally put 'embrowns' because Hardy uses it to wonderful effect in the opening sentence of 'The Return of the Native' . . . The memory of Hardy seduced me into saying 'tranter' instead of 'carter' or 'wagoner' for 'carrettier'. 120

from the Greek of Theocritus (*c.*315–*c.*250 BC)

THE ENCHANTRESS (first published in Arthur Bliss, *The Enchantress: Scena for Contralto and Orchestra*, London: Novello & Company, 1951). HR's 'free adaptation' of a passage from the Second Idyll of Theocritus as an operatic *scena*, set by Sir Arthur Bliss for the contralto Kathleen Ferrier in 1951, and performed by her with the BBC orchestra under Charles Groves, Manchester, April 1952. 122

PART VI Early poems, drafts and fragments (1935–1986)

GREEN, SPLEEN, & C.: (?) a sequence, 1935–1940. Text from a typescript, 7 ff., autograph emendations, HR's autograph datings; found among the author's papers. 'Dull Sonnet' was preserved separately, in a folder seemingly containing 'rejects'—poems not to be included in what may have been a projected collection.   127

DE ARTE POETICA (? c.1940). Text from an unidentified cutting among HR's papers, with the title 'Ars Poetae' altered as here, and with numerous (? provisional) autograph revisions in the author's earliest—i.e. 1940s—hand. Lines 53–59 are cancelled, but as no replacement lines are offered they have been restored here.   130

THE FUTURE (? 1947–1954). Text from undated typescript, autograph emendations; there is an autograph draft with numerous variants among the author's papers. Note in notebook of c.1954:

> A feeling, almost night-marish, and not *dilettante*, that some scenes about me now I may not see again until I am an old man. The pressure of others' thoughts on such themes: Hardy's especially I suppose. This must be frank introspection—it cannot be made into a thing. [On facing page:] This might fill out, or even absorb, or be absorbed in, poem about the 'future', begun many years ago.   133

PSYCHOLOGICAL WARFARE (?1950–1970). Typed draft with autograph emendations, 7 ff.; autograph note at head: 'USE THIS COPY but v. pp. 6 & 7 of the other', is in shaky late hand. Earlier (?) typed drafts show minor variants. A number '5.' preceding the title would seem to indicate that this poem was once intended to form part of the sequence *Lessons of the War* (cf. Part II above) of 1970—indeed, the author in conversation in the 1970s mentioned that such an afterpiece had been composed.   135

THE CHÂTEAU (? 1950s). Text from autograph fair copy. Earlier (?) autograph drafts are titled variously, 'On the Terrace', 'The Façade'.   143

A GOOD DREAM (? 1950s). Text from autograph fair copy. Earlier (?) autograph drafts contain minor variants.   145

THE INTRUDER (? 1950s). Text from an incomplete autograph draft which breaks off at line 16 of section IV, and is completed here from an earlier rough draft. (HR has noted on the latter, in a late hand: 'The state of my eyesight is worse than I can ever have expected'.) Two other autograph drafts exist among the author's papers, the earliest—identified by HR as 'the first version'—with the title 'The Return'.   146

THE SOUND OF HORSES' HOOVES (? 1950s–1985), fragment. Text from typescript of opening 8 lines, with autograph emendations, continued in (?) later, inconsecutive autograph draft. One leaf has the bracketed note: 'There shd be one rather lengthier subject of conversation to bring the poem to a gentle climax', and still another the lines, 'and there seemed no cause for wonder, / In the simple and boundless fact that we loved each other'. There are two (?) earlier drafts, one titled 'First Sight', another in a (?) 1954 notebook. HR seemingly

163

returned to the poem much later, noting on 10 March 1985: 'And today it seemed to me that an attack around the *scalpiccio* [. . .] bit would be right. After that, silence and polite disregard between the two. [. . .] But how end the thing?' 150

THE VOW (? 1950s–1985), (?) fragment. Text from an autograph fair copy; there are two other (?) earlier autograph drafts. H R's note dated 10 March 1985: 'The other day thinking of "The Vow" the determined phrase "Never weep" came up. This may be the beginning: of the end of that piece and may make me more actively able to interfere in the last part.' 153

[L'ENVOI] 'They told him, with reassurance' (? 1970s–1980s). Text from an undated autograph fragment, found loose in a notebook from the (?) 1950s, though the hand is evidently that of a much later date. Its placement at the end of the present volume relates to its content rather than the possible date of its composition. 154

INDEX OF FIRST LINES

166